This book is fictional history.

My love of Hawaii and history motivated me to write this series of books. This story takes place from the end of World War I to the end of World War II. Most of the facts remain true, however in this timeline Queen Maili Kaanapali reigns over the Hawaiian Islands.

I want to thank my family and friends who supported and encouraged me throughout this long process.

I specifically want to thank my main editor Amy for her dedication to getting this book ready for my target goal of middle and high school students. I hope everyone, young and old will enjoy it too.

I'd like to thank my illustrator Grace for another beautiful cover, along with a big thank you to Marci, Mike, and Debi for pre-reading the book for me.

Lastly, I want to thank my dear friend Reginna Maili for her inspiration, and allowing me to use her lovely and regal image on the cover.

The other books in the series can be found on Amazon:

Hawaiian State: A Story of King David Kalakaua

Hawaiian Legacy : A Story of Queen Lydia Kamake'eha

Soon to be released:

Hawaiian Dynasty : A Story of the Twin Queens

Hawaiian Legend

A Story of Maili, the Maui Pebble Queen

Chapter 1 - Attack on Pearl Harbor

East of Haleiwa, Dec. 7, 1941

Privates Elliott and Lockard were working the graveyard shift at Opana Point. Opana is the northernmost point of Oahu. It was a little before 7 a.m. They were working at the newest technological station in the military. It was a radar facility. They picked up a huge blip and called headquarters in Honolulu. Lieutenant Tyler told them it was a group of B-17s coming in from California and not to worry about it. Elliott shrugged his shoulders and turned off the radar device, and they ended their shift.

Twenty-five miles to the south, Queen Maili's twin daughters, Princess Elizabeth and Princess Bethany, had begun their annual pineapple picking. The twins loved their annual trek to the pineapple fields for Christmas. They loved getting away from the palace and the city. They loved the smell of fresh pineapples as they strolled through the pineapple fields. Most of all, they loved this special weekend with their closest friends, the Schildmeyers.

Queen Maili decided not to attend this year due to suspicions of possible terrorist attacks by the Japanese on American and Hawaiian military sites on Oahu. Maili remained at Iolani Palace to assist if a crisis emerged. Kenneth Junior, or Kenny, was the oldest Schildmeyer. He had the privilege and responsibility of getting his ohana to the fields and back home safely. Kenny's younger siblings included Emily 21, Charlie 20, James 19, and Hannah 16. The twins and Emily were born just a few months apart, just like their mothers, and were just as close.

As always, the princesses had bodyguards with them. Today, Tatu and Izzy were on duty. The days of grass skirts were over unless an official occasion required traditional garb. Prince Austen's purchases of several Tommy guns for the security team made Tatu and Izzy very capable of defending the princesses should trouble arise. For an early December morning, it was warm and beautiful. The sun had been up for a bit, and light, puffy clouds floated gently across the Hawaiian sky.

Hannah asked naively, "Kenny, will God be upset with us for missing church today?"

Kenny looked upward to the blue sky and thought carefully about how to defend their actions, saying, "Hannah, you worry too much. I think we'll be okay with this one time. Besides, I think the princesses commanded us to be here."

Bethany chuckled and gently slapped Kenny's shoulder, "Kenny, we did not 'command' you to be here. Don't let him fool you, Hannah. However, we are so glad we have kept this tradition all of these years."

Bethany put her arm around Charlie, kissed her cheek, and said, "I love your dress. It's so festive."

Charlie asked, "May I play a song on my ukulele for the Princess?" and Bethany smiled and nodded.

James asked the princess with a silly grin, "What, you don't like my pants?"

Bethany looked back at James and said with a smirk, "Oh, yes, James. They are … opala!"

James smiled, showing his teeth, and said, "Mahalo."

"Yes, Charlie, please play something seasonal." Bethany said.

"I just learned this one from Dinah Shore. It's called *The Merry Christmas Polka.*" Charlie began to pick and sing.

Bethany clapped joyfully, "Oh, Charlie, that is adorable."

Elizabeth was already out in the fields, scoping out her favorite pineapple. "Hey everyone, remember to take two! That goes for you, Tatu and Izzy! "

Tatu raised his eyebrows and said, "Yes, Your Majesty. As you wish. Tatu looked at Izzy as they started to pick two ripe ones off the plants.

Tatu cut it open, and they shared a slice. "Ono!" They both chuckled.

Tatu had to wipe the juice off his face.

An hour before...

Outside the mouth of Pearl Harbor, the destroyer USS Ward was alerted that an enemy submarine was attempting to enter Pearl Harbor. It quickly sank the midget submarine at 6:45 a.m., firing what would be the first shots of World War II. Unfortunately, this news did not alert the rest of the Navy.

Back in Haleiwa...

The royal siblings and the Schildmeyers, loaded up with Christmas pineapples, began to meander through the fields back to their vehicles.

"Where's James?" Kenny asked.

"I'm down here, crawling between the plants. No one noticed I was hiding for like five minutes," James said, disappointed. James stood and noticed a shape far away. He pointed out to the northern horizon. "Hey, do you see that?"

The group stopped as they heard a faint buzz of airplane engines in the distance. They looked out onto the horizon, and coming from the north appeared to be more than one hundred airplanes!

Kenny was a pilot in the Hawaiian military. "Ummm, folks, this is not good. Those are not American planes!"

Princess Bethany curiously asked, "Kenny, how can you tell?"

We have been training for this for years. Those are Japanese Zeros! This is bad! Then, in a panic, "EVERYBODY, GET TO THE CARS!"

Tatu and Izzy sprinted to the vehicles and retrieved their machine guns from the trunk. Tatu yelled at everybody to get down and stay behind the cars. "Maybe they won't see us!"

Tatu and Izzy both pointed their 40-caliber Tommy Guns toward the planes. Zero after Zero flew over. There were well over one hundred, plus another wave could be seen flying over the western point of Oahu. The planes were flying very low and fast. They could see the pilots in their cockpits. Kenny was right. There were large red circles on the wings. They were Japanese planes.

Kenny shouted at Izzy, "I need to get to Haleiwa airport right away to get my plane up! You take the princesses into the jungle until it's safe. I'll call the queen and let her know! Izzy responded with the Shaka sign.

Kenny drove as fast as he could to a local farm while the rest of the group hid behind the vehicle. A Japanese farmer was watching the planes fly over. "Those bastards are committing a sneak attack on Pearl Harbor!"

Kenny shouted, "Can I use your telephone?"

The farmer said, "Yes, of course."

The royals and their friends continued to twist their bodies together behind the car, as they lay as low as possible.

Izzy raised his machine gun slowly. "Tatu, when the last plane goes by, I am going to shoot just in front of the propeller. You aim for the front of the cockpit." As the last fighter plane was rumbling overhead, "Three, two, one." Izzy and Tatu sprang up and unloaded 50 rounds at the Japanese pilot. Several bullets hit the plane. "Let's get in the car and go!" The seven passengers crowded into the car and sped off down the dusty farm road toward the jungle for cover. It was nearly a mile from the farm. Elizabeth was driving as fast as the car could go.

Pilot Nishikaichi took several rounds to his Zero and was wounded in the shoulder. Leaking fuel, he decided to head back to his carrier. He turned right, flying over the pineapple fields, and watched as the royals were attempting to speed away. Not knowing if he would make it back, he decided to shoot at the civilians below.

James looked back and yelled, "Speed up, Elizabeth; he's right behind us!" Izzy and Tatu now realize shooting at the plane was a mistake.

Izzy shouted, "STOP THE CAR! EVERYONE RUN!"

Elizabeth slammed on the brakes. Everyone got out and ran in different directions. Izzy screamed, "HIDE IN THE PINEAPPLES!"

Pilot Nishikaichi was surprised at how all the passengers disappeared so quickly. He decided to shoot up the car anyway. As he pulled his trigger, a short burst of bullets rang out. Then the machine gun jammed from the damage from Izzy and Tatu's Tommy Guns. The Zero flew by at 100 miles per hour. Izzy and Tatu fired off another burst until they ran out of ammunition. Several more bullets hit the Zero. Ichiwa was losing fuel and knew he wouldn't make it back.

Kenny called Iolani Palace, and after a moment, Queen Maili picked up. "Queen Maili! There is an emergency! You must get to safety!"

Maili asked, "Are the girls okay?"

"Yes, Izzy is taking them into the jungle for a couple of days. Japanese planes are heading your way! You need to get to safety now!"

Maili heard the buzz of several planes and then a huge BOOM! An incredible explosion rocked the palace.

Savita, one of the Queen's guards, ran up to Maili. "Your Majesty, we must get you to the shelter now!"

Maili dropped the phone and ran. Kenny got back into his car and drove to Haleiwa Airfield, where his plane was already getting prepared for battle.

"Captain Schildmeyer, your plane is fueled up and armed. It's ready when you are," Sergeant Jones yelled.

Back in Honolulu, Savita was pulling Queen Maili by the hand until they got to the bunker underneath the palace grounds. "You will be safe here, Your Majesty! Stay here until the bombing stops!"

Savita ran back into the palace to arm himself. In the bunker waiting for Maili was her only female bodyguard, Somoa. Maili called her Sommy.

Queen Maili asked, "Sommy, what have you heard?" Sommy locked the bunker hatch.

"Your Majesty, it's the Japanese! Sommy replied.

The furious queen shouted, "I can't believe they did it again!"

Chapter 2 - Maili's Coronation

Iolani Palace, Honolulu, November 13, 1917

Many decades prior...

Maili (pronounced Mi lee) Grace Baitmen Kaanapali Chamberlain was 27 years old. She was about to be the youngest monarch in Hawaii in nearly one hundred years.

Queen Lydia had passed away just two days prior. It was imperative for the safety and longevity of the throne that Maili be crowned quickly. Even though there hadn't been a coup attempt in years, Maili and her new cabinet did not want to give any motivation for evildoers, whether they were foreign or domestic. Maili knew that just months before, Czar Nicholas of Russia had been forced to abdicate his throne. If it could happen to him, it could happen to any monarch.

Princess Maili had grown into a stunning young woman. American magazines like *American Woman, Country Life in America*, and later *National Geographic* realized that her face on the cover increased sales. As queen, sales would be sure to increase. Most of these publications were in attendance at the coronation.

Lizzy stood behind Maili as they both looked in the mirror, "Your Majesty, you look gorgeous! I am sure the ancestors are jealous; they cannot watch your coronation in person."

Maili looked into Lizzy's eyes in the mirror's reflection and smiled. "I love you, Lizzy. You've been my best friend since I can remember. I have to tell you, I am so scared." She began to cry.

"Oh, Maili. Why? Queen Lydia prepared you your entire life for this moment."

Maili exhaled and wiped her tears away. "Auntie's voice is always in my head. I just… wish she were here to see this."

Lizzy looked up and smiled, "Oh, I think she is."

Maili continued to look down, "Well, now that it's here, I just feel overwhelmed. I am not sure I will be able to do what Auntie Lydia would want, or, for that matter, what is best for Hawaii."

Lizzy tiptoed around Maili and kneeled, "Maili! Do you remember what Queen Lydia told you on the first day of school?"

"Yes, I do. Be brave. Be strong. Be kind."

"Well, you are all of those things and more," Lizzy grabbed her hand. "You have a strong cabinet. You have Austen, and you have me and Ryan."

Maili glanced over her shoulder to see if anyone was around, "Lizzy. I've never said this to anyone… I don't think Austen has my best interest or Hawaii's in his heart."

"Why do you say that?"

"He meets with a lot of people in secret. When I ask him for his advice, he always gives me a weird look. It's just a feeling I get and can't shake."

Lizzy looked her in the eyes and said, "Listen to me, My Queen. Let's not worry about any of that now. Take a deep breath, and let's go out there and change the world, just like the ancestors foretold."

The future queen and her best friend embraced. Lizzy asked, "You know what's weird?"

"What's that, my dear?" Maili wiped away another tear.

"I've called you 'Princess' my entire life. That was the first time I called you, 'My Queen'. I like the sound of that." Lizzy nodded and smiled.

Maili smiled, "I do too. I love you so much, Elizabeth Doel. I think it's about time you got an official title. Like 'Royal Advisor', or 'The Queen's Chamberlain.' Chamberlain means Chief of the Castle."

"Oh! I like the sound of that. Elizabeth Doel, the Queen's Chamberlain."

Waiting on the palace grounds below were thousands of people. Most of them were Hawaiian. Many were the children that Maili had helped in her reign as a princess. Others were reporters from around the world, from *National Geographic, the New York Times,* and even as far away as *the London Times* were in attendance. Even though the Great War still raged, readers around the globe were ready for some good news. Maili's coronation was just what many women were waiting for. Maili wasn't a household name just yet, but her popularity was growing. Readers were curious if Maili could fight off aggressors and improve Hawaii's economy and way of life.

Just like Queen Lydia before her, Maili's bodyguard, Maka, sounded the conch shell. Wooooooooooooooooo. It was time to begin. The crowd became silent. Only a few cries from young pepes; being held in their mother's arms.

Hawaiian drums began to play. Izzy walked on stage with his ukulele and began to sing a verse in Hawaiian, then in English, about the history of the Hawaiian people. Izzy told the story of the first Polynesians from the Marquesas Islands. He told the story of the Menehune. He told the story of

Kauai and its jungles. He told the story of Molokai, its amazing waterfall, Kalaupapa, and the first hula dance on Molokai. He told the story of Maui and Haleakala. He told the story of the Big Island and the arrival of the first Westerner, Captain Cook. Izzy told the story of the Great Kamehameha and how he was the first king to unite the islands. He told the story of King David and the attempted coups. He told the story of how Princess Lydia sang Aloha Oe. He told the tragic story of the birth of Maili and how she lost Keilani. He told the story of Mail's work for the children of Hawaii. He told the story of the ancestors, who were watching from above. He told the story of the Maui Pebble Queen, who, like Hawaii, was small but strong. Izzy ended his melodic yet hypnotizing song with this phrase: "The BEST IS YET TO COME!

Maili's guards, Somoa, Tatu, Izzy, and Maka, all yelled a loud Polynesian, "YEEEEE HUUUUUU!"

Then thousands of people yelled back, "ALOOOOOO HAAAAA!"

Maili walked through the mahogany doors and onto the balcony railing and waved. An explosion of cheers began. People were yelling her name. People were clapping. People were crying. The energy of the crowd overwhelmed Maili for a moment. Austen held her hand tightly. "It is time to address your subjects, My Queen."

Many Hawaiians had never seen Maili before, even though Maili had made several public appearances. She had attended many ceremonies and had visited every island. Still, not everyone on the islands had seen her in person.

The Hawaiians and the press were surprised, and several in attendance were struck by her beauty. Maili had olive skin, long wavy dark hair, large, piercing dark brown eyes, full lips, and a smile that could stop any kane or wahine in their tracks.

As Maili began to speak, the crowd was mesmerized.

Maili was the first Hawaiian monarch to address the crowd with the assistance of a microphone and speakers. This was another one of the many new inventions to come to the islands. Maili's voice was nothing like Queen Lydia's. Lydia had a lovely, soothing, and natural tone. Lydia was a great singer. Maili loved to sing, but her voice often cracked at higher pitches. The poor girl was tone-deaf. Maili's higher-pitched voice was still endearing to the Hawaiians.

Maili began to speak, "My fellow Hawaiians. Today... is a bittersweet moment for me. My beloved Queen Lydia has made her final journey to be with her ancestors. I want you to know that Queen Lydia raised me, adopted me, and prepared me my entire life for this moment. The blood of King Kamehameha the Great runs through my veins. I always knew this day would come, but my heart still breaks for my Auntie Lydia." Maili looked into the crowd and saw many of their faces streaked with tears.

"I promise you this: I will defend Hawaii by any means necessary."

Across the street on a second-floor balcony, two men watched and listened to Maili. One was wearing a Japanese military uniform. One was wearing the black clothes of a Chinese peasant, yet the clothes were new and recently laundered.

They looked through a pair of binoculars. "She is stunning!"

Lizzy was panning the crowd, admiring the love for her new queen and best friend, when she looked out across the street onto the balcony where a Japanese soldier and Chinese gentleman were sitting. She whispered to herself, "Oh my God! I don't believe it!"

Maili continued, "I will continue to support the needs of the children of Hawaii. We will continue to push our schools to be the best in the world!" The crowd cheered.

"We will continue to allow technology to come to Hawaii that betters our lives, yet always embrace the traditions that made Hawaii great." The speakers popped and cracked, which irritated many of the listeners.

We will continue to protect our jungles, our waterfalls, our reefs, and our beaches. Tourists come here with the expectation that Hawaii is the most beautiful place on earth. We must be good shepherds of our islands and need to keep them that way." The people cheered even louder.

Lastly, in keeping with the spirit of my great Auntie, Queen Lydia, and her sister, Princess Anna, we will continue to uphold the rights of women's suffrage here in Hawaii. Like in America, women are starting to vote in local elections. I want this for Hawaii!" The wahines went berserk!

"I am proposing a 'Bill of Rights' as they have in America. I want more involvement in local issues to be solved by the local people. I will continue to rule Hawaii as a kingdom, but I want mayors, chiefs, and villagers to have a say in the day-to-day challenges. So I end with my best "ALLLLOOOO HA"; her voice cracked. The crowd laughed along with Maili as she laughed at herself.

Austen brought over the official yet humble crown. Prince Austen placed it on her head. "May I present to you, Queen Maili Grace Kaanapali Chamberlain Kamaka 'eha!" Several thousand people erupted with shouts of joy!

Maili walked back to the microphone and said, "May I present to you the official royal choir. Please join us in singing the song my Auntie wrote, Aloha Oe."

Maili waved and said, "A hui hou, ka kou!"

Chapter 3 - Maili's Bodyguards

Security Office, Iolani Palace, November 14, 1917

Izzy called the meeting of the security team to order. Izzy had been promoted to Chief of Security upon the death of Koa years ago. "Aloha everybody. I'd like to welcome Savita to the team. Please introduce yourself and tell us your story."

Savita was 6'2" and over 300 pounds. "Aloha. I was born in Tonga. My parents brought me here when I was seven. So I went through the Hawaiian education system. I speak Tongan, English, Hawaiian, and Pidgin, Bruddahs. I used to cut lava rocks for a living."

Tatu remarked, "So that's how you got to be so damn big. Haole." The group laughed again.

"Oh, Cousin, for sure. I train in karate with my Japanese uncle. I did a little bouncing periodically at some bars in Waikiki. I am quite comfortable dealing with crowds." Savita proudly responded.

Maka asked, "You have an Ohana, Cousin?"

"Happily married with five kids."

Sommy shot back, OOOOOH, Cousin, that's plenty."

"My wife thinks so too," he smiled. "But we practice all the time for more." The group laughed again.

Izzy sat down and scooted in his chair. "Ok. We have no idea how many lolos are out there. So let's look sharp for a while. When the queen travels, Sommy, we will need you to inspect the wahine's rooms. In return for extra travel, we will give you more days off."

"Gotcha boss." Sommy snapped and pointed back at Izzy.

"I want everyone to have firearms any time we are out and about. The abdication of Czar Nicholas has me spooked. With the war winding down, governments and terrorists might get desperate and try something rash. So we will always have two guards next to the queen and one to protect our rear."

Tatu raised his hand and said, "Izzy, I was wondering if maybe we should hire a few more agents to protect the queen when we are out on the streets?"

Izzy responded, "We have a lean budget; the guards outside will have to assist us from time to time. So let's get out there and protect Her Majesty."

Sommy popped out of her seat and patted Tatu on the back. Izzy pulled Sommy's long ponytail as he walked by and smiled. Sommy asked Tatu, "How about some beers for pau hana? Bring the wife, and I'll bring Afa. He's been home with the kids all day. He's about to pull his hair out. He says he needs 'adult time'."

Tatu thought for a second: "You know what? I think Laveni would love to come."

Izzy made a motion for Maka to come over and whispered, "I have seen the way you have been looking at the queen. That needs to stop immediately! If I sense any inappropriate behavior, you will be terminated. Do I make myself clear?"

Maka looked surprised and said, "I mean nothing inappropriate towards Her Majesty. It's just..."

Izzy cut him off. "I know Cousin; she's beautiful. It doesn't matter. Look at it this way. We must protect the 'title', not the person per se. One day, we may have another queen. I was here for Lydia, and now for Maili. Look beyond the outside of the queen, as difficult as that might be. Am I understood, Maka?"

"Perfectly."

Sommy and Tatu witnessed the conversation and knew it wasn't good. Sommy approached Maka and asked, "Does someone need a hug?"

Maka was quite muscular. He was 5'10" and weighed 250 pounds. He had a chiseled jaw and was a decent-looking man. He stared down at Sommy as she got closer. Maka slowly curled his arm and slapped his bicep. "You couldn't handle a hug from these tiger sharks!"

Sommy took on that challenge. She ran up into Maka's space and wrapped her arms around him. She squeezed him so hard that he started coughing. She lifted him and shook him. "Ok! OK! Put me down, you Amazon!"

Sommy shook her head while keeping eye contact with Maka. She curled both arms to flex her biceps and strutted out of the room. Tatu was bent over, laughing. Maka tried to breathe. "Oh, my goodness, Cousin. That wahine is strong!"

Tatu asked, "Is everything okay with Izzy?"

"I guess so. He saw me gawking at the queen. Cousin, she is so adorable. Sometimes I can't help myself. Prince Austen is one lucky fellow."

Tatu put his hand on Maka's shoulder and said, "Oh, I understand. I have been around here for some time now. Queen Maili gets prettier every day, but I swore to protect her. We are lucky we don't have an 'ewa queen, right?" Maka nodded.

Chapter 4 - Christmas Pineapples

South of Haleiwa, Oahu, December 20, 1917

This was Maili's first Christmas without Lydia. Maili was determined to keep many of Lydia's traditions alive. Picking the annual Christmas pineapple was one of them. Maili now includes Austen in this tradition. Christmas at Iolani Palace became a blend of American, British, and Hawaiian customs.

Along with the queen were Lizzy and Ryan Schildmeyer. As always, the security detail was close behind. Today, Sommy and Tatu provided protection. "Your Highness, how does one pick the perfect Christmas pineapple?" Austen inquired with his British accent.

"Prince Consort, are you being serious?" Queen Maili responded in her pretend British accent.

"Of course, my love. There are a million pineapples here, and I haven't a clue what I'm looking for."

Ryan chimed in, "Me neither, Your Majesty."

Lizzy placed her hands on her hips and said, "Ryan Schildmeyer, I have told you multiple times what to do."

"Maybe I want our queen to tell me, just to be sure," Ryan said with a smile.

Lizzy huffed, put her nose in the air, and turned away in jest.

The queen began to joyfully lecture, "Gentlemen, let the old professional tell you how to pick the best Christmas pineapple. First, look for yellow. The more yellow the pineapple, the better. Then I squeeze it. It must be firm, yet give a little. It's too firm; it's underripe. It's too soft; it's overripe. Third, I smell its bottom. There should be a lovely aroma."

Austen said under his breath to Ryan, "So the queen enjoys sniffing bottoms? That would be some headline."

Ryan burst out laughing. "What is so funny?" Lizzy asked with her arms crossed.

"Oh, nothing, my dear," Ryan said as he turned away.

Maili crossed her arms too. "If I know these two lolo troublemakers, it was probably naughty."

Austen motioned Ryan away from the indignant ladies. "How about this one?" Ryan leaned over and said, "Oh, let me smell its bottom." Austen chuckled.

Maili motioned Lizzy over, saying, "Let's go over here and pick out some good ones. You know, My Queen, this is a very special pineapple Christmas." Lizzy continued to shop.

Maili continued with a fake British accent, "And why is that Elizabeth, Chamberlain of Iolani Palace?"

"This will be the last one for me and Ryan." Lizzy's face appeared emotionless.

"WHAT?" Maili raised her voice, which got the attention of Sommy and Tatu.

"Well," Lizzy looked down, "this is our last pineapple Christmas for the two of us because next year we will have another person joining us." Maili wasn't picking up on Lizzy's clues. "Your Majesty, I am hapai!" Lizzy began to cry. Maili's frown slowly turned into a wide smile as it began sinking in.

Then her eyes opened wide, and she shouted as loudly as she could, "YEEEEEE HUUUUU!"

Austen looked over in shock. "What the blazes?" Ryan put his hand on the prince's shoulder and said, "Lizzy must have told her we were expecting."

"You're what? Good job, old chap! When's the due date?"

"We think it's the middle of June. Lizzy swears it's a boy. I don't know how women know such things. They shook hands and jogged over to the girls.

The girls were blubbering joyfully as Lizzy's tummy was suddenly noticeable. Maili placed her hand gently on Lizzy's stomach.

Tatu looked over at Sommy and asked, "What are you crying about?"

Sommy wiped away her tears and said, Oh, you wouldn't understand Tatu. Every time Afa and I were expecting, it was such a joyous time."

The group had picked their fair share of pineapples. Maili and Lizzy were discussing boy names. They were about to head back to Honolulu when Austen motioned Ryan over to the trunk of one of the Pierce Arrow Model 66s. It carried seven passengers and had a trunk. Austen opened it up. Inside the trunk was the newest machine gun. There were two Thompson 'Tommy' guns.

"Wow!" Ryan spoke softly. "What the heck are those?"

"These are the latest machine guns. The Thompson factory hasn't released them to the public yet. They are letting me try them out and expect a thorough evaluation. Do you want to shoot a few rounds?"

"Oh, let's do that!" Ryan said it excitedly.

Maili approached the vehicle and asked, "And just what are you two up to now?"

Prince Austen said, "Look, Your Majesty! These are the newest machine guns. Ryan and I are going to try them out."

"Here?" The queen asked.

"There's no one around." He motioned for Sommy and Tatu to come over. "I want you both to shoot these. If you like them, I'd like to equip the entire team with them."

Tatu walked over and said, "Impressive!"

Austen brought one out, and everyone stood back. "You attach this drum right here. Pull back this lever, and let'er rip." Austen told everyone to cover their ears, pulled the trigger, and let off ten quick rounds into the jungle with a loud RATTATATATATATAT! "Goodness gracious, this thing kicks, but what a weapon!"

Sommy, come here and give it a try. Sommy hustled over and said, "Yes, sir. This seems fun."

Austen kept giving tips until everyone fired off a few rounds; even the queen fired a short burst. "Well, that was invigorating, but my shoulder hurts."

Austen smiled and said, "Your Majesty, I believe your guards could hold off a small army if they were all equipped with these Johnnies."

An hour later, Maili and Lizzy were riding in the back seat and giggling most of the way home about the prospect of a new Schildmeyer. Suddenly,

Maili's mood changed. She lowered her voice. "Something is bothering me about Austen".

Lizzy leaned in and asked, "What is it, Maili?"

"Austen is making these weapons deals, and I have no idea what he is doing. I hate to say this, but I don't trust him. As a husband, yes; as the prince," she said, shaking her head.

Maili leaned on Lizzy's shoulder and dozed off for a bit. When the royal motorcade made its way onto the palace grounds, the group got out of their vehicles.

Maili stretched, yawned, and looked at the palace. "We need more decorations. I miss the Christmases back in England. The snow and the cold air gave Christmas such a different feel."

Lizzy walked up to the queen and put her head on her shoulder. "I miss the California ones too. Everyone had a Christmas tree. Maybe we could decorate a palm tree? Or put a wreath on the front door? Or, better yet, a nativity scene? After all, it is the celebration of Baby Jesus."

Maili asked, "What's the nativity scene?"

"Oh, Your Majesty, it is a depiction of Jesus being born in the manger."

"Oh yes. Let's do that." Maili smiled joyfully.

Ryan asked, "Is there any way we can get a pine tree? Back in California, we decorated our Christmas tree. It pays homage to Martin Luther, who they say was the first to decorate a Christmas tree."

Austen sauntered over to the girls and said, "Perhaps we could place some red bows around the light poles?"

Maili clapped excitedly. "Now we are getting in the spirit! What about this? The guards could wear red shirts."

Tafa said under his breath, "Oh, joy."

Sommy elbowed him. The Christmas of 1917 was the beginning of years of happy Christmas memories and blended traditions for the Chamberlains and Schildmeyers.

Chapter 5 - Maili and Po visit Molokai

Kalaupapa, March 20, 1918.

Dear Queen Maili,

You may not remember me, but we met years ago in Honolulu when you were a princess. My name is Jack Skott. I used to work for Queen Lydia and the Department of Health in Oahu. My job was to test and escort lepers to Molokai.

As fate would have it, I contracted the disease as well. I have been here for many years now.

My dearest friend, Jo San, has a dying request. She understands you are friends with her brother, Po San. She has little time left and requests that he make one last visit to Kalaupapa.

*Is there any way for you to send him to Kalaupapa
as soon as possible?*

With great admiration and respect,

Jack Skott

Maili read the letter, folded it, looked at Lizzy, and
sighed. She spoke to her bodyguard, who was with
her in the chamber, and said, "Maka, do you
remember where Po San lives? I know he returned
to Hawaii."

"Your Majesty, if I recall, he lives close to the new
canal, just a few blocks from here. Shall I bring
him here?"

"Please ask him to come, and that is extremely
urgent!"

"I will leave immediately, My Queen."

Lizzy was listening to the conversation: "My
Queen, Po has been back in Hawaii for several
years, and he hasn't made one attempt to contact
you? I find that so odd."

"Well, our secret service has been watching him.
He has political ties with the communists here and

in China. I do not trust him, but he has done nothing wrong, yet."

An hour later...

Maka and Po entered Queen Maili's chamber.

"Po! Oh, my goodness. It's been almost six years!" It is so nice to see you." Maili said as she approached Po.

Po did not make eye contact. His face was turned down as he frowned.

"Well, Po, unfortunately I have very sad news. Jo's friend Jack wrote to me and said Jo does not have much time. May I escort you to Kalaupapa so you can see her one last time?"

Po shook his head and said, "Yes". He appeared to be irritated. He took a deep breath and asked, "When can we leave?"

"I will have *the Kalakaua* ready first thing tomorrow morning. Let's say 8 o'clock." Maili moved towards Po to show empathy.

Po stepped back and said, "I will be at Pearl Harbor at sunrise tomorrow." Po did not bow. He simply turned and left. Maka followed behind him to see him out.

Sommy, who had been present for the entire meeting, said, "He seems rather ungrateful, Your Majesty."

"I am sure his mind is spinning."

"May I speak freely, Your Majesty?"

"Of course, Sommy."

"If he disrespects you again like that in front of me, I will stuff that haole into the opala."

"Mahalo, Sommy, but that will not be necessary."

The next morning ...

The Pacific Ocean off the Molokai Coast

Po was sitting on a bench near the front of the ship. Queen Maili approached Po and asked, "Is this seat taken?" She said it with a smile.

Po continued to stare forward, saying, "You are the queen. Do as you please."

Maili looked back at Sommy, hoping she didn't hear. Maili sat down next to Po. Cloud cover blocked the sun this day. Maili was chilled and threw on her shawl. "Po, may I ask what is bothering you? Are you mad at me?"

Po sat quietly for a moment. He took a deep breath and said, "May I be honest with the queen?"

"Po, it's me, Maili. Of course you can."

"Maili, you never apologized for slapping me. If you recall that night, you kissed me first. I did not deserve that humiliation. I saved Lizzy from Hideki's advances, and what thanks did I get? A slap from the princess in front of the entire party."

"Po, I can't say I'm sorry enough. I was so upset that we were all leaving each other. I was mad that you drank. I was extremely mad at Hideki, and you embarrassed me in front of everyone. I just snapped."

Po sighed. "So your apology comes with excuses? I just wish the world was different."

"How so?"

"My thoughts shouldn't concern you, Maili." Po said rudely.

Maili became irritated with Po's disrespect. "What happened to you in China? You used to be a happy and pleasant person!"

Po looked at her with some fear for the very first time.

"As my childhood friend, I want you to be happy. I am willing to apologize for something I did years ago as a child. I'm sorry, Po! That will have to do. Accept it, or don't!"

Maili got up and stormed away. Sommy watched the angry queen stomp back to the bridge. Sommy marched over to Po, stuck her finger in his face and said, "Listen here, little man, if I ever hear you disrespect my queen again, I will tie a weight around your skinny little ankle and throw you overboard! Do I make myself clear?"

"Perfectly!" Po continued to stare straight ahead.

Sommy was six feet tall and well over two hundred pounds. She was probably the strongest and largest wahine in Hawaii. She was not making an idle threat.

Jo's residence, Kalaupapa, a few hours later...

Jack met the queen and Po at the docks. They addressed the queen's admirers as Po ran straight over to Jo's place. Death was a common occurrence in Kalaupapa. There was little fanfare on this visit, yet a visit from the queen was always an exciting day.

Po and Maili sat at Jo's bedside. Jo was quite groggy and appeared to be unsure of where she was. Po asked, "Jo, are you ok?" Jo was covered with a blanket. Her face seemed aged but untouched by leprosy.

Jo turned to her brother and asked, "Po, is that you? You made it."

"Yes, Sister. I brought the queen with me. I told you I knew her."

Jo looked to the other side of the bed and smiled at the queen. "Oh my! Aren't you beautiful?" Maili smiled back.

Po spoke as if Maili was not there, "I am still mad at Queen Lydia for sending you here, Jo. You did not deserve this—this hell on earth. While the rich live free in Hawaii, the poor get sent here—to this prison. Now that we have this Hapa Queen, it will not get any better."

Jack looked horrified! "How could Po disrespect the queen like that?" he wondered.

Po continued to escalate the situation, "Jo, do you remember when Queen Lydia burned down Chinatown and robbed Father of his ability to make a decent wage?"

Maili was furious. She was not going to tolerate Po's disrespect. Jack followed her as she stormed out of the door.

Po grabbed Jo's hand. "I will avenge you, sister. You and all those imprisoned here. My life's goal is to end the Hawaiian Monarchy!"

"Oh, Po. Why do you have so much anger? I have been so happy here. I met the love of my life." She looked at Jack's photograph and smiled. "People have always treated me kindly here."

Po could not let go of his rage, "Jo, I am sorry to say this now; both mother and father have passed away this year. They worked themselves to death just trying to buy a bowl of rice. The amount of food the queen throws out every day could feed half of their village. This must end!"

Jo struggled to catch her breath. "My infection is draining me, brother. I cut my foot and didn't discover it until it was too late. I am dying, Po. I just want you to be happy."

"I will be happy when Maili loses the throne. Jo, when I was in China, I met this amazing man called Mao Zedong. He showed me how the rich will always take advantage of the poor. Action is the only way to straighten out the world. I plan on taking action."

"Oh, Po. I need to sleep for a while."

Queen Maili quickened her pace as she hurried to the pier. She looked at no one. The lepers were shocked at her lack of aloha spirit.

She told Sommy, "Let's leave!"

Sommy looked back for Po and said, "What about the little man?"

Maili gritted her teeth. "He can find his own way back," Maili and Sommy marched down the new ramp. This was one of the upgrades Maili insisted upon when she became queen. This enabled leper children to safely make it up the pier. Within a minute, they were on the new motorized dinghy and puttering away back to *The Kalakaua*.

Sommy asked Maili, "May I ask what upset you, My Queen?"

"That ungrateful and resentful... after everything we have done for the lepers, he blames me for their suffering! He actually called me a hapa in front of his dying sister."

"If I had known that, My Queen, I would have thrown him into the ocean."

"It is ok. He is persona non grata." Maili tried to convince herself she didn't care about Po.

Chapter 6 - Hideki and WWI

Tokyo, Japan, June 1, 1912

Several years in the past...

Hideki Yamamoto graduated from the Imperial Japanese Military Academy as number one in his class. His mastery of Japanese, weaponry, secret codes, and military history sparked the interest of the academy commander. It was just weeks before graduation in 1912 when Hideki got a message from his company leader, "HAI! Lieutenant Yamamoto, Commander Yakatsu has called you to headquarters immediately."

Hideki was studying for his final exams and needed to get dressed to meet with the commander. Within minutes, Hideki was dressed to perfection. Not a button was out of place.

Hideki marched quickly and impeccably over to headquarters. Yakatsu was addressing several high-ranking officers; they waved Hideki in, saying, "Please have a seat, Lieutenant."

Hideki was perspiring and hoping the commander would not notice. He had never been in the commander's office before. Hideki was praying this was not about the hazing incident.

The officers all sat behind Hideki. The commander sat down and leaned in, saying, "Lieutenant, at ease. The reason you were invited here is a good thing." The commander had realized Hideki was nervous. "I want to personally congratulate you for being number one in your class. The committee here has a special request for you."

Hideki nodded. "Yes, Commander. Anything for the Emperor."

"We believe Pearl Harbor is going to one day be the most important port in the entire Pacific. We believe that you are the perfect candidate for our plan to obtain Pearl Harbor. We are aware of your relationship with the queen. Your mission is of the utmost importance. The Americans are attempting to gain more access there. We need to turn the tide against American imperialism. We believe in a slow but constant push for control of Pearl Harbor until the time is right to take it."

"I am honored, Commander." Hideki said.

"Lieutenant, I want to read you a letter I received that was addressed to you.

Cadet Yamamoto,

The gods have spoken to me.

It gives me great pleasure that they chose you as the man to achieve our goal in Operation Kaizen.

I ask, as your emperor, for you to live your life to fulfill your destiny. Operation Kaizen will require that you give your life to the achievement of the following:

Use teamwork to achieve your goal.

Use personal discipline to achieve your goal.

Keep your morale high to achieve your goal.

Keep a quality circle of acquaintances to achieve your goal.

Always suggest improvements to achieve your goal.

Your goal, Lieutenant, is to overthrow the monarchy of Hawaii and assist the Empire of Japan in controlling Pearl Harbor before the Americans gain control.

With sincere respect,

Emperor Meiji"

"So you see, Lieutenant, it is not just us. It is your emperor who knows your destiny. I know you will make us all proud. Please follow Colonel Makura, and he will give you all of the necessary information."

Hideki proudly accepted his mission. For the next several years, Hideki would prepare to assist the emperor of Japan and the fascists in their attempt to overthrow the Hawaiian monarchy and control Pearl Harbor.

Both the United States and Japan entered the Great War at different times and for different reasons.

Japan decided in 1914 to honor its alliance with Great Britain and declare war on Germany. However, most advisors to the emperor believed Germany would defeat Great Britain. Japan knew that Germany had colonies in China. Japan needed those colonies for natural resources for its tiny island nation.

Japan secretly used this reasoning to join the Triple Alliance. It would be the beginning of forty years of imperialism and fascism. Hideki's nationalism would blind his love for Maili and Hawaii.

By 1915, the United States was shipping supplies to the Allies. Most Americans preferred to remain neutral. However, after a series of U-boat attacks, including the sinking of the Lusitania, Americans were leaning towards war. However, it was the Zimmerman Telegram that swayed Americans to fight. Germany's secret plan to have Mexico attack the United States pushed Americans into the conflict.

Chapter 7- Commander Mulsen and *the Kamehameha*

Celebes Sea, North of Indonesia, April 10, 1918

Commander Patrick Mulsen had been given the dangerous task of sailing on *the Kamehame* to Australia, Indonesia, and the Philippines to gather weapons and supplies for Hawaii.

When Queen Lydia's health was waning, she wanted to have enough weapons for Princess Maili, should World War I come to Hawaii after she passed. *The Kamehameha* had traded Hawaiian fruit and sugar in exchange for weapons and spices in Australia and Indonesia. Captain Dale had many of these missions, but today he was unaware he was being watched as he sailed through the Celebes Sea towards Manila.

Queen Maili, along with Lizzy and her security, were discussing a whale festival in the upcoming months. The mood was light. Suddenly, Prince Consort Austen stormed into Queen Maili's office and said, "Excuse me, Your Highness, but I need to have an urgent discussion with you about *The Kamehameha*!"

Austen rarely called Maili anything besides her name. She knew this was urgent. "Yes, Austen. What seems to be the problem?"

"You sent Commander Mulsen to Australia for weapons without notifying me." Austen said it angrily.

"Austen! Mind your tone! I am the Queen of Hawaii!" The couple has been fighting more often these days.

After hearing the altercation, Izzy and Maka approached the couple.

Austen took a deep breath. "My Queen, I have been negotiating for months now with Australia for weapons."

Maili motioned for the guards to stand down. "Listen, Austen, I am doing what I think is best for Hawaii, not your pocket book."

Austen had a look of disgust for a moment and said, "Whatever do you mean, My Queen?"

"Austen, don't play dumb with me. I know you have been profiting and secretly stockpiling weapons on Lanai. I have seen to it that Commander Mulsen will be dealing with our armaments from here on out."

"We can discuss that later; right now, *the Kamehameha* is in grave danger, along with its crew!" Austen raised his voice again.

Izzy took a step closer to Austen. "What do you mean?" the queen asked.

"If you had asked for my guidance, I could have told you there are Uboats in that region. Three merchant ships have already been sunk."

Maili shook her head in disbelief. "Why would the Germans be in this hemisphere?"

"My Queen. Some people are calling this a world war. There is fighting everywhere."

"That makes no sense, Austen."

"Let me try to explain. Uboats, or unterseeaboots, were made by the hundreds leading up to the war. I know this because I sold the Germans some materials for torpedoes."

"That is how you made your money prior to the war?" Maili asked.

"Well yes. Unfortunately, the Germans mistakenly sank the French ship Sussex, in 1916. They pledged not to sink any more civilian ships to keep America out of the war."

Maili asked, "How did that turn out?"

"The realization that America was shipping weapons on civilian ships forced Germany to begin sinking merchant ships again. The Lustania and Arabic were sunk, killing over 100 Americans. This war crime, along with the Zimmerman Telegram that Germany sent to Mexico, so infuriated Americans that President Wilson persuaded the Senate to declare war on Germany last week." Austen explained.

"So why is *the Kamehameha* in danger?" Maili asked.

"My Queen, Hawaii is allied with the Americans. The Germans were determined to prevent any weapons from landing in any country not allied with the Central Powers. Just last year, German U-boats became an effective weapon in this Great War. These small submarines are hunting down ships they deem a danger to the fatherland. Today, we know that there are at least two in the South Pacific. They refueled in Singapore, and their secret was exposed."

Maili walked over to the open window and looked upon her garden so no one could see her fear. "Let's get word to Captain Dale to get home immediately.

Back in the Celebes Sea...

As *the Kamehameha* was traveling north towards the Philippines, two Uboats, named U69 and U70, were sailing together, watching *the Kamehameha*. The Uboats had been watching them since Australia. Their mission was not to allow any weapons to reach the Philippines.

Captain Hans Hisher on board the U70 told his first officer, "Apparently that ship cannot travel faster than 10 knots. We will continue to stay below the surface until it is dark, then signal U69 to catch up to the ship's port side. We will place two torpedoes into it. Those weapons must not get to Manila."

Chapter 8- The Great War Ends

Iolani Palace, November 11, 1918.

On the eleventh hour of the eleventh day of the eleventh month, 1918, the Great War ended.

All told, over ten million soldiers were slaughtered. This loss of life would later be called *the Lost Generation*. Nearly ten million civilians were killed—numbers never seen before in history.

Another twenty million soldiers were wounded. Many of those lost limbs, lost their vision, lost their hearing, and lost their sanity.

Queen Maili was strolling along the royal gardens with Lizzy and Ryan when Tatu was carrying something in his hand and approached Queen Maili. He had a grand smile. "What do you have there, Tatu?"

"I bring great news, Your Majesty!" Tatu handed Maili a copy of the Honolulu Times.

She opened up the front page. Maili placed her hand over her mouth and began to cry happy tears. "Finally, Tatu! At last, the great slaughter is over! I am so relieved."

"I thought that would bring you great joy," Tatu remarked.

Crown Prince Austen ran through the gardens, yelling, "Maili! Did you hear the news?"

Maili ran to Austen and said, "Yes, Austen. The war is finally over! I think we should declare a day of mourning, remembrance, and celebration.

"Oh, I agree, Your Majesty. That is a superb idea." Austen joyfully agreed. The group jogged with excitement back to the palace to begin the planning.

Maili's guard, Izzy, opened the doors and said, "Your Highness, your noon appointment is here." Maili looked at Austen and said, "Please stay for this meeting. I think you'll enjoy it."

Izzy announced, "Queen Maili, may I introduce you to the Secretary of the United States Navy, Franklin Roosevelt, and his top aide, Walt Underson?"

Roosevelt stopped and bowed. "It is my honor to finally meet you, Queen Maili. As Secretary of the U.S. Navy, I want you to know that we want to keep alive Queen Lydia's dream of making Pearl Harbor the strongest and most secure port in the Pacific. Now that the war is over, perhaps we will have many years of peace. However, I believe in peace through strength."

Austen introduced himself. "Oh yes, your reputation precedes you, Prince Austen!" Roosevelt said. Austen quickly glanced over at Maili.

Maili understood what that meant. Maili asked Roosevelt and Mr. Underson to sit. They began collaborating on how the military could make agreements between the two countries. The conversation lasted for hours and until dinner. Maili was very concerned. "I hope that the United States will be welcome as long as they promise not to expand anywhere in Hawaii without the specific permission of the queen."

Roosevelt began to review, "We promise to maintain Pearl for the next fifty years. We will dredge. We will maintain all facilities at our cost, as long as we can use Pearl Harbor to port our ships. We also agree to establish multiple airstrips. We see the use of military aircraft becoming more important in the future. This will be a boom for your economy, Your Highness. Are we in agreement?"

Austen interjected, "We will have the ability to secure armaments for our military."

Roosevelt looked at the queen and said, "As you know, Prince Chamberlain, that has been going on for some time. We hope that will continue."

Maili looked at Austen with confusion. Not wanting to embarrass him in front of Roosevelt, she let the topic go.

Franklin's wife, Eleanor, joined the group. The two couples celebrated with other guests in the ballroom. They danced well into the night. It was the start of a long-lasting relationship between Queen Maili and Franklin Roosevelt. Sadly, it would be the last time Franklin would dance with Eleanor, as polio would soon strike him down, depriving him of the ability to walk, run, or dance again.

As Maili and Austen retired to the chamber for the night, Maili turned to Austen and asked, "What is going on with the armaments, Austen? I had no idea what Franklin was talking about, and it has been going on for some time."Maili rarely raised her voice toward Austen.

 Austen shushed the queen. This angered her even more.

"Do not shush me, Austen! Tell me, what is going on? Where are all of these weapons?"

"Maili, the military has control of almost all of them. I did not want to bother you with such things. I do have some hidden away on Lanai in a secret location."

"So secret that the Queen of Hawaii isn't supposed to know of their whereabouts? Well, I already do!"

"I was eventually going to tell you everything, my dear."

"Don't,'my dear me', Austen. You do not have the authority to do such things. This will stop immediately! Am I understood?"

Izzy and Sommy were outside their door, quietly listening. "Yes, Your Majesty. I will be transparent from now on."

"Perhaps you didn't understand me, Austen. This ends now. You will no longer purchase any weapons without my full knowledge and consent.

Maili turned and stormed off. Austen remained there, wondering how he could continue to secretly weaponize 'his' military in Hawaii and benefit Great Britain. Sommy and Izzy exchanged glances, and Sommy pantomimed her punching Austen.

Chapter 9 - The Roaring Twenties and Hollywood

The Moana Hotel, Waikiki Beach, February 10, 1920

Tourism, along with the military buildup in Hawaii, was improving the economy seemingly instantaneously.

Thousands of Americans and Australians began vacationing in Honolulu. The word spread about the elite accommodations and near-perfect weather, no matter the season. American military personnel began to marry the locals, and families were beginning to create a demand for homes and schools.

The queen and her staff were celebrating Hawaii's success. Maili had arranged for a beefed-up police presence at the Moana so she could reward her security team for all that they had done for the crown. The security team and her staff were treated to dinner, drinks, and dancing. All of the windows on the lower floor were opened to allow the fresh ocean breeze to blow through the restaurant. The sun was setting and the sky turned orange, which lit the room and everyone in it in a citrus tone.

After dinner, the guards all slipped away, which was curious to Maili. Maili and Austen were dancing along with the other guests. Most of them were impressed with Maili and Austen's new dance, the tango.

Suddenly, the band stopped playing, and the emcee asked everyone to take a seat. "Tonight, Your Majesty and honored guests, we have a special performance for you. Please put your hands together for the 'Graceful Guards'!"

People clapped. Izzy came bouncing out with a grass skirt and grass anklets. He carried a torch and yelled at the top of his voice, "ALOOOOO HA!"

The crowd responded with an "ALOOOO HA!" in return.

"Tonight, My Queen and Prince, Kanes and wahines, we have a special performance, which I am sure you will enjoy. Please welcome the Graceful Guards!" Tatu, Maka, Savita, and Sommy all stomped out, yelling tribal grunts and chants.

Maili sat back in her chair, giggling and applauding. The guards had their spears and stomped as they stabbed the air. Loud drums sounded like thunder as a tribal beat entranced the crowd. Izzy told stories of how ancient Polynesians came to Hawaii and created a new culture. All the guards were wearing grass skirts, except for Sommy. She wore a bright green moo moo and haku with bright red flowers.

Then suddenly, there was silence. Sommy moved gracefully to center stage. The other Kanes left the stage. A spotlight hit Sommy, and the restaurant went dark. Sommy approached the microphone and said, "I would like to dedicate this to our gorgeous Queen Maili and her beloved Auntie Lydia.

She began singing Aloha Oe. People froze. It was as if an angel were singing. Her soft, sweet voice struck right into people's hearts. When the song was over, not a sound could be heard except for the sniffles throughout the room.

Suddenly, Queen Maili jumped up, clapping and yelling, "HANA HOU! The audience was brought back to its senses and gave Sommy a standing ovation.

Later, each Kane guard performed a history of their culture.

The night was a tremendous success and such a treasured evening for Maili, who thanked the guards profusely. This performance announced what would be an amazing decade for Hawaii.

What would be a decade to remember, the 1920's symbolized the American and Hawaiian spirit. Prohibition in America created a greater demand for alcohol as speakeasies opened all over the country. Hawaii decided to make alcohol a reason to visit. Alcohol remained legal on the islands. The Mai Tai, the Blue Hawaiian, the Pina Colada, and the Rum Bowl were even more reasons for tourists to visit Hawaii.

The first projection movie theater was erected in 1922. The movie theater called *The Princess* was considered a Nickelodeon but showed movies on a large screen.

During the late showing of *Nosferatu*, Queen Maili took Maka and Sommy with her. Rumors were swirling that this was a new genre of movie called 'horror'. They were told not to watch it without friends. Nosferatu was the first of many vampire movies. Locals had never seen such a scary movie.

Maili sat between Maka and Sommy. Queen Maili had been escorted along with her guards up to the VIP Suite by the theater manager. There, in a private suite, the three audience members could watch the movie in the dark without worrying about interacting with the general public.

As the vampire crept around the castle, Sommy got so scared she asked Maili, "My Queen, may I hold your arm? Maili was scared too. "Of course, but I think I'm going to hold onto your arm." Maili pulled Sommy in close.

The two grown men leaned into each other and held on like frightened children. Maka leaned forward, looking over at the wahines, and said, "Really?"

A scary scene made Sommy and Maili jump out of their chairs and scream along with the rest of the audience. They could not wait for the movie to end. As they walked through the lobby, Sommy was still hanging on to the queen. "My Queen, I have never been so scared."

Maka chimed in, "Sommy, you are the strongest woman I know. You are afraid of a make-believe monster?" Maka motioned to indicate to Sommy that she was still holding on to the queen.

"Oh, Your Majesty, I apologize for hanging on to you. My apologies."

Maili chuckled. "Well, mahalo for a strong arm to hold onto.

Maka broke protocol by saying, "If you wanted a strong arm, you could have held onto mine, Your Highness."

Sommy looked over and said, "She wanted a strong arm, Maka!"

"Your Majesty, please wait here with the weak-armed one and let me go get our motor."

Maili looked at Maka and smiled. "Sommy sure does tease you a lot."

"Oh, Your Majesty, she teases all of us. But she's a sweetheart under all that muscle."

Maka smiled at the queen. Maili looked deep into Maka's eyes for the first time. The late-night breeze brought a cool wind, which broke the gaze. "You look chilled, My Queen; let me get you your shawl." Maka ran over to the motorcar and grabbed the queen's shawl.

Maili was embarrassed that she had gotten caught up in the moment. She reminded herself that she was the queen and still a married queen.

The movie had transported her to a new world. As more technology infiltrated Hawaiian culture, the queen, like so many other Hawaiians, was being forced into a quickly changing planet.

Chapter 10 - Three Babies

Waikiki Beach, April 1, 1920.

Queen Maili and Lizzy were sitting in the warm sand outside of the Moana Hotel. The waves in Waikiki in the spring are quite mild. Swells continued to wash upon the shore and slide back into the Pacific as the sun gleamed down on them. Occasionally, the sun hit just perfectly and temporarily blinded the wahines with a brief flash.

The friends noticed that the sun and sky appeared different today. The sky appeared a darker blue, as if there was a thin cloud cover, but there wasn't a cloud in the sky. Lizzy glanced quickly at the sun, and to her surprise, she could tell half of it was covered.

"Oh my, it appears we are experiencing a solar eclipse! I just noticed the birds aren't singing either." Lizzy said.

Maili listened. "Well, what do you know? They are silent today. It feels like dusk. So weird."

"Now I remember reading something about it in *The Times*."

"Lizzy", Maili paused for a moment and looked into her eyes. "I have a question. It is totally unrelated to the eclipse."

"Yes, My Queen, what is it?"

"Please call me Maili. I need a friend right now."

"Oh, my goodness, Maili. What is the matter?" Lizzy looked around to see if everyone was far enough away not to hear.

"How do you know if you're expecting?" Maili began to tear up.

Lizzy jumped to her knees, leaned in close to Maili's face, and whispered, "Are you hapai?"

Maili whispered back, "I think so. I've skipped my period for two months! And this morning... it felt like two butterflies were flapping their wings in my stomach."

"Oh my! Maili!" Lizzy whispered loudly, "You are expecting! Why the tears?"

"Oh, Lizzy. I think you know how I feel about Austen. We have not been in love for some time. I like him less each time I see his face. However, I am so excited about being a mother like you. You are such a great role model."

"Well, Maili, guess what? I am expecting too!" Lizzy said it excitedly.

Maili screamed, "YEEE HUUU! The queen of Hawaii and her best friend were bouncing up and down from their knees and began hugging like schoolgirls.

Savita looked at Izzy and whispered, "What the hell is going on, Izzy?"

"Oh, they have known each other since they were children. Sometimes they get a little... lolo." Izzy made a circle motion near his ear.

Savita looked at Izzy and said, "Don't ever do that to me. So help me; I will punch you."

"No worries, Cousin. I'm good. I'm not a fan of the sand anyway. When my wife, Iki, and I roll around in the sand, I get sand in all kinds of bad places." Izzy chuckled at his own joke.

After laughing for minutes, Lizzy said, "Hey, wait a minute! You said you felt two butterflies?"

"Is that not normal?" Maili wondered aloud.

"Well, Maili, this is my second, and I have felt one butterfly, but not two! Maybe you're having twins!" Lizzy screamed.

Maili looked back at Izzy and Savita. Izzy ran to Maili and asked, "Your Majesty, is this true?"

"Thanks, big mouth!" Maili snarled at Lizzy.

Lizzy covered her mouth. "I am so sorry. I am just so ecstatic!"

Maili looked at Izzy and said, "Well, I guess you would find out sooner or later. I am expecting."

Izzy placed both hands in his mouth and screamed at the top of his lungs, "YEEEE HUUUU!" This got the attention of the onlookers.

Maili said, "I want to be the one to tell Sommy. Let's go over to her house now before the rumors begin to swirl." Maili became distracted by something shiny on the beach as she scooped up a handful of sand. Two small black pebbles rose to the top. She shifted her thoughts to her parents. She wondered if she would make a good mother. Maili pondered how life would be for her two daughters. Maili somehow felt she would have girls.

Izzy asked, "May I assist you up the beach?"

"I'm hapai Izzy, not helpless," she said with a smile.

Lizzy asked, "Does Austen know?"

Maili looked at Lizzy as she lowered her brow and thought, "Frankly, I could care less if he knows," but answered, "Not yet."

The royal motorcade rolled up to Sommy's residence.

"Mommy, there are some people in cars out front," Tutu shouted at his mother.

Sommy was in the middle of making dinner. She cleaned her hands and walked out front to see who was visiting. "Who is it?" Tutu asked.

"Son, it is our queen! Be on your best behavior, please."

Sommy approached the motorcade as Maili and Lizzy got out of the car, smiling. Savita and Izzy were smiling too. "What is going on?" Sommy asked Izzy as she squinted her eyes.

"Oh, it is not for me to say, Sommy."

Maili and Lizzy skipped up to Sommy, holding hands like they did as childhood friends.

"This is lolo," Sommy said.

Lizzy and Maili continued to stare at Sommy with silly grins. "You are freaking me out!" said Sommy.

"Sommy, I wanted to be the first to tell you." She looked at Lizzy and said, "Lizzy and I are expecting!" Maili said it happily.

Sommy's eyes got big. "WHAT? YEEEE HUUUU!" she screamed at the top of her lungs. Sommy took a large step forward. "May I hug the queen?"

Lizzy and Maili pounced on Sommy as they all jumped up and down with glee.

Sommy had to wipe her tears away and say, "Please come in for dinner. I was just getting it ready. We have so much to talk about. AFA! Come out here!"

Afa was a large man too. He bowed, "Aloha, my queen. What an honor to have you here in our ohana's hale."

"Aloha, Afa." Maili shook his hand. "We adore your wife."

Afa smirked. "Yah, she's okay."

Lizzy said, "There's more! The queen is having twins!"

Sommy yelled again, "YEEE HUUU!" I am so very happy! Two more pebbles from our beautiful pebble queen."

Chapter 11 - Po and Hideki plan their revenge.

Honolulu, June 7, 1920

Po received a letter from Hideki while he was stranded on Molokai. Hideki's spies had informed him that Queen Maili had stranded him there.

Po remained with his sister, Jo, until she took her last breath. His grief and anger grew as the days passed. He decided to make the strenuous hike over the mountains to begin his new journey. He would hike until he arrived in Kaunakakai.

Po was sloshing through the trail over the mountain near Waikolu Overlook. He was by himself with no weapons. Several large thunderclouds had dropped heavy rain and then fled off into the distance. The jungle was dense, the air was thick, and tropical birds could be heard singing their songs. As if a light switch had been flicked off, it became dark. A large, thick cloud covered the sun. The tropical breeze ceased, and the birds became silent. It was difficult to see into the kaleidoscope of green leaves intertwining from the ground up onto the canopy.

Po stopped to catch his breath. His skin quickly became covered with goose bumps. He could feel someone watching him. Po tried to get his eyes to adjust, but the faint light and thick foliage made it difficult to see more than 20 feet ahead.

A twig snapped, and Po's head darted to his left. Through a small opening in the jungle, there were several pairs of eyes very low to the ground. Po panicked! He had no idea what types of creatures they were, and he had nothing to defend himself.

He slowly began sliding through the mud backward. He would look over his shoulder to help guide him around the corner. After slowly retreating for 20 yards, Po turned and ran as fast as he could down the trail until he couldn't run another step. The creatures did not follow.

Po continued down the mountain, occasionally looking back. However, it wouldn't take long for Po to forget his ordeal and continue with his obsession to raise a group of followers to help him dethrone Queen Maili.

Communist Vladimir Lenin referred to his minions as 'useful idiots'. These were people whom Lenin could persuade to commit acts of violence to increase political pressure on his rivals. They would march, throw rocks, and burn buildings if asked. Po learned this tactic from his college comrade, Mao Zedong, while in Hong Kong.

Po recruited the poorest and most bitter villagers from Molokai. He knew one day he would be able to travel back to Oahu and begin his communist coup d'etat.

Hideki quietly observed Pearl Harbor for months. His goal was *kaizen, the* slow but constant improvement of his plan. Hideki watched as he saw Japanese businesses grow in the Honolulu area. He would introduce himself to as many Japanese sympathizers as possible. Hideki never gave away his plan, yet he believed he would one day have enough support to create chaos on the island. This would allow the Japanese military to make a sneak attack on Pearl Harbor.

Through Hideki's spies, he learned of the altercation between Maili and Po. Hideki needed more support and believed Po could help. Hideki planned a secret meeting with Po when he arrived on Oahu.

Hideki was wearing civilian clothes and waited at the back of the bar. Po opened the door wearing his traditional black clothes. Hideki could only see his silhouette at first. Po looked around the bar. It took a moment for his eyes to adjust. Small windows allowed small beams of the sun to light up the smoky air. Po recognized Hideki. Hideki waved him over.

"Have a seat, old friend." Hideki pulled a chair out.

"So we are friends again? I hope that means you have forgiven me for the going-away party." Po spoke quietly.

Hideki signaled to the bartender, "What can I get you to drink, Po?"

"Sake is fine." Po scooted his chair closer to the table.

"A bottle of sake, please," Hideki said to the bartender. "I was an ass that night, no doubt. I deserved it. So tell me, Po. What happened on Molokai between you and the queen?"

"Wow! Bad news travels fast." Po looked off across the restaurant.

"It has been a few months, but I have friends close to the monarchy, and they hear things."

"Hideki, while I was in China, I met a man called Mao Zedong. He changed my life. He showed me that the only way to get political change is through action, not talk."

"What does that have to do with Molokai, and what type of change are you looking for, Po?"

"My parents died dirt poor, Hideki. Their lifetime of strenuous labor meant everything to my parents and nothing to the rich people of Hawaii or the queen. I expressed my feelings openly, and the queen did not like it. I want to carry out Lenin's and Mao's dream of a worldwide restructuring of the capitalist system. Take it from the greedy, wealthy people and redistribute it to the workers that deserve it."

Hideki played along, saying, "I like where you are going with that thought. In Japan, I saw the same. I saw how the Europeans took advantage of Asian people. This, too, must stop. Perhaps we can help one another?"

"Perhaps, Hideki." The bartender delivered the sake. Hideki poured some for Po. "What do you have in mind?"

"I understand you have brought some supporters with you." This caught Po off guard. He turned to Hideki with a surprised look.

"Yes, Po. I know almost everything that goes on here in Honolulu. I know you want to overthrow the monarchy. I also want Japan to control these islands. I think that if inferior people, like the Americans, the British, and these deplorable Hawaiians, are in charge of your system, it doesn't matter what it is. We in Nippon believe the Japanese are the supreme race. We believe we will control the entire hemisphere one day. Island by island, we will rule the Pacific, just like the British have done for centuries."

"Nippon?" Po asked.

"That is our true name. It means the land of the rising sun. One day, Po, mark my words; we will rule the entire Pacific and much of Asia. Perhaps China too." Hideki looked out of the corner of his eye, waiting for a response.

Po sipped his sake and said, "I have no quarrel with the Japanese, yet. However, I will do everything I can to destroy this monarchy and murder every single landowner and business owner if that's what it takes to give the worker a fair shake in life."

"Whoa, easy there, tiger. You want to murder Maili?"

"My childhood friend, Maili, no. The queen of Hawaii, yes." Po stared into his cup.

"Would you commit to my plan if I helped you achieve your plan?" Hideki whispered.

Po turned to Hideki and said, "I will do anything to make that happen! Hideki, my family is all gone now. I want revenge!"

"Outstanding. I will need to meet your team as soon as possible. Agreed?" Hideki asked.

"Yes, Hideki, I agree. Hey, I am starving; can you buy me dinner?"

"Wow, a broke communist! Shocking." Hideki signaled the waiter to bring a menu. "Po, I do not wish to burst your bubble, but you are aware that communism cannot work." Hideki lectured. "We studied it in the academy. Human nature never changes. People need incentives to work. Money is the best incentive."

"I disagree, Hideki. The gun is the best incentive." Po countered.

"You have a point. By the way, I am very sorry for your loss. You had a horrible year." Hideki placed his hand on Po's shoulder.

"My depression has evolved into anger. I will make my feelings known soon enough." Po said as he looked off.

"I am worried about you, Po, on many levels. I want you to be happy. You've had a rough life. You need to celebrate life from time to time."

"I will celebrate when I am with my parents and sister in heaven," Po said joyfully. "May I order some teriyaki chicken and rice?"

"Waiter." Po snapped for the young man to come over to the table and said, "We would like an order of teriyaki chicken with rice and two orders of tuna with a bowl of rice, please." Hideki handed back the menus.

"Raw fish? That is a custom I just can't get used to. I like my food cooked." Po teased.

"You see, Po, that's the spirit. Laugh a little. You know, I was thinking about the first time we met the princess. That was a crazy day."

"You should have let her drown," Po said with an evil grin.

Chapter 12 - Remembering

The Queen's Garden, Iolani, Honolulu, September 10, 1920

Little Kenny Junior was running around the garden. Sommy was in hot pursuit. "I'm gonna getcha! I'm gonna getcha."

Kenny giggled as he ran. Lizzy and Maili were sitting on a bench in the shade. The very pregnant queen rested a lot these days. Lizzy adjusted her towel to start feeding Emily.

Maili looked into the lush gardens. The walking paths were as thick and green as the jungles of Manoa. "Lizzy, I'm scared."

"Maili, what's the matter?" Lizzy turned to her.

Maili placed her hands around her large tummy. "My mother died giving birth to me. For the first time in my life... I have been thinking about death. What if I don't make it? I don't want Austen to take the twins back to England."

"My Queen, neither of those things is going to happen. Your mother's pregnancy and yours are two separate events. You will have the best doctors in Hawaii at your beck and call. Millions of mothers around the world are just like us and give normal births every day. Please do not worry."

"Promise me, Lizzy, that if something happens, you will take care of it. "I hope they will be queens one day."

"So you believe you are having girls?" Lizzy asked excitedly.

"Well, it's kind of like you said; I dream of girls all the time. I am assuming that's the ancestors talking to me. I was thinking of their names last night, and I think I have them picked out."

"What does Austen have to say about this?"

Maili looked at Lizzy through the corner of her eye and smirked, "The first one will be Elizabeth Lydia Kamaka'eha Ka'anapali. The second one will be Bethany Maile Kamaka'eha Ka'anapali."

"Bethany?" Lizzy asked.

"That's Austen's mother's name. She is a sweet woman, and I figured since they will not have the Chamberlain name, at least I could keep his mother's name alive."

Lizzy said aloud, "Elizabeth Lydia, oh my God! You are naming your daughter after me?"

"Really Lizzy? That surprises you? The two most important women in my life are you and Auntie Lydia. Now I am glad I am having two, or she would have one long name." Maili laughed at her joke. "And Maile is after my cousin in La Haina. Lizzy, I was just thinking of our weddings the other day. I was so happy. Austen seemed so perfect. I believe he wants to do something nefarious here in

Hawaii. I truly believe his loyalties are with his money and England."

"Well, my queen, then he is a fool. Ryan and I are ecstatic about the name we gave our girl, Emily Maili Schildmeyer." Lizzy leaned her head on Maili's shoulder. "I was reflecting the other day about the first time we met Po and Hideki. They were such brave and sweet boys. My, how different they turned out."

Maili sighed. "I wonder what Hideki is doing. I haven't seen him since the coronation. I assume that little communist Po is still on Molokai, trying to blame me for all of his problems. He must have a puka in his head."

Lizzy sat up quickly as Kenny tripped and fell.

Sommy looked back at the nervous mom and said, "Oh, he's ok, babies bounce."

"I just do not understand how the communists cannot believe in God and believe that everyone is equal. If that were the case, why would anyone strive to be better?" Lizzy asked.

Maili continued to watch Kenny run around, saying, "I've been doing a lot of reading lately on Karl Marx and Vladimir Lenin. It makes sense to those who are without. They don't have much to lose, so they are willing to take from others and, as Maili Air quoted, redistribute to the less fortunate. I was also thinking about the conversation we had as children. About you being more Hawaiian than I am. I think about that all of the time, oddly."

"Oh dear, why?" Lizzy sat up again.

"For years, especially in England, I was starting to feel less and less Hawaiian. I changed my name. After Auntie passed and she saw all of her ancestors, it was an epiphany."

"My Queen, you rule over the most beautiful place on earth, I'd wager. Hawaii is worth fighting for. You have dedicated yourself to kuleana. Our culture is worth fighting for, too. I am not sure you believe in Jesus, but the Hawaiian gods, or Jesus Christ himself, do look over you. You are the epitome of what a Hawaiian wahine is."

"Is it wrong to believe in Jesus and the Hawaiian gods?" Maybe they work together somehow." Maili wondered.

Lizzy thought for a moment, "Who knows, maybe Jesus, Pele, and Lydia are all up in heaven now telling stories."

Maili remembered her wedding day again: "Remember what a happy day my wedding day was? I miss being happy like that."

"Oh, happy days will return, My Queen. Children bring more happiness and pride than you can even imagine." Lizzy rubbed her shoulder.

Maili looked up into the sky, wondering where Lydia was, and then she felt a very strange pain in her abdomen. "OHH!" Maili grabbed her tummy.

Lizzy asked, "Maili, are you alright?"

"I don't know. I've never felt anything like that before. What does going into labor feel like?"

Sommy ran over with Kenny and said, "Your Highness, are you going into labor?"

"I don't know. It kind of felt like something was squeezing my entire abdomen for a second. Oh dear, I think I just peed myself. Now what?" Maili began to worry.

Lizzy's eyes got big. "Your water just broke."

Sommy was a veteran after bearing five children: "The first one is always the scariest because of the unknown. Let's get you up and back to the palace. I will call Old Doctor Lau." Sommy was holding onto Kenny and, with her other hand, easily helped Maili off the bench, saying, "Easy now."

The contractions began to come more quickly and regularly. Doctor Lau brought his entire nursing staff with him, knowing twins could be a more difficult delivery.

The medical staff and Lizzy remained with Maili in a downstairs bedroom. Austen, Ryan, Izzy, Maka, Tatu, Savita, and Sommy all remained outside, pacing around the main entrance. The rumor got out, and the press was waiting on the grounds.

The delivery suddenly became life-threatening, and Maili began to bleed heavily. Lizzy prayed, "Please God, help Maili come through this." Doctor Lau asked Lizzy to leave the room, as they were about to perform an emergency cesarean section to save the girls and the queen.

The bedroom door opened, and everyone stopped, hoping for exciting news. Lizzy looked down and sighed. "The queen is bleeding, and they need to perform an emergency cesarean section to save the girls and her majesty."

Austen bent over and placed his hands on his knees. The security team all began to tear up. Ryan spoke up and encouraged everyone: "Please, let's all pray for a quick and safe delivery." They all bowed their heads and became silent. Members of the press could see through the glass windows that something was wrong, and a growing buzz of chatter could be heard inside the palace.

A nurse ran through the door and towards the telephone. "We need an ambulance at Iolani Palace immediately!" She ran back into the room. Tatu became light-headed and sat down. Austen began contorting his face, trying not to cry.

A few, but very long, minutes went by.

Austen asked, "Do you hear that? It's a crying baby!"

Old Doctor Lau shuffled over to each nurse whispering out and said, "Prince Austen, the good news is the twin girls are beautiful and healthy. The queen made it through surgery. However, from my experience after this type of surgery, she will probably never have any more children."

Ryan comforted his friend by laying his hand on his back.

"We have ordered an ambulance. I would like the queen to remain at the Queen's Hospital for a few days. She is unconscious. You will be able to see the babies when the gurney arrives."

The ambulance arrived shortly, and the paramedics were shown into the birthing room. An ambulance headed to Iolani created a mass of curious seekers. Hundreds quickly gathered around the palace. Maili was wheeled out of the birthing room. Two nurses brought the girls by. They stopped in front of the group so everyone could see.

Elizabeth was a tiny brown baby. She was yawning along with Bethany, who was a bit fairer. As if on cue, both girls opened their eyes. Everyone stopped talking. They were in shock! Elizabeth's eyes were blue. Bright blue. Her eyes were as blue as the ocean on a sunny day. Bethany's eyes were green. Bright green. Emerald green. It was as if every adult in the room was in a trance. The nurses carried them to the ambulance, and they drove off.

Austen looked at Ryan and said, "Did I just see what I think I saw?"

The group laughed together out of nervousness. All of them began talking about the babies' eyes and patting Austen on the back.

Sommy hugged Izzy and said, "Those princesses are going to be special. They are gifts from the gods."

Chapter 13 - Po's Revenge

Mikuni's Restaurant, Honolulu, September 11, 1920

Po scurried over to Hideki's favorite restaurant at noon. Po guessed Hideki would be at this Japanese eatery. Po stopped at the top of the short stairs again, searching for his comrade. Hideki was already dining with some Japanese associates at a back table.

Po reached the group and asked, "Can we talk in private?"

"Please have a seat and have some lunch, Po. These are all of my associates. I keep no secrets from them."

Po grabbed a chair from another table and snapped for the waiter to come over. He ordered his favorite teriyaki dish.

Po lowered his voice and leaned into the group. "As I am sure you are aware, the queen and the princesses are at the Queen's Hospital. In her current state, I believe she is vulnerable."

Hideki looked at his colleagues and said, "Yes, Po. What are you thinking?"

"I have some volunteers to assist me in murdering the queen, the princesses, and the prince," Po said joyfully.

The Japanese men at the table stopped eating. They looked at Hideki like his friend was crazy. "Whoa. Wait a minute, Po. Don't you think that is a bit severe?"

"I have been patient, Hideki. It is time to strike. Getting to the palace is too difficult. We can wait until the prince is visiting. With my four men, we subdued the two guards, burst into the room, and murdered them all in mere seconds."

Hideki's colleague, Hiro, interjected, "I like the way you think, Po. However, consider this: murdering the queen will surely bring in the Americans to fill the power vacuum. We cannot allow that. Shortly, Japan will be ready to invade and overthrow the Hawaiians, but America is another story."

"Hideki, you told me if I helped you, you'd help me. I need some more weapons."

"So the communists can't afford weapons either," Hideki said with spite.

"Hideki!" Po raised his voice and asked, "Are you with me or not?"

"Po, you need to relax. Do not come into my place and disrespect me in front of my associates." Heads started to turn in their direction.

Po sat silently, staring across the room. His meal came, and he began to wolf it down. The Japanese men stacked their empty plates and thought, "What a pig!"

They watched Po devour his lunch. He barely took a breath.

"I will do what I must. We will find a way." He got up and stormed out of the restaurant.

"Where do you know this animal from?" Hiro asked.

"Unfortunately, he was a childhood acquaintance. He went to China and got involved with Mao Zedong, a communist revolutionary who was studying Lenin. The poor soul is misguided and bitter because his sister was sent to Kalaupapa. He has no money. He earns no money. All he does now is think about killing the queen. I think he is going to ruin our plan, gentlemen."

The next morning...

Po and his comrades waited for Prince Austen to enter the hospital. Two men armed with pistols and two men armed with knives entered the hospital from different directions. The Chinese assassins saw the guards standing outside the queen's door. Po pulled his weapon out of his pants. From the other direction, two other men with knives approached the guards.

When the Chinese communists were within ten feet of the guards, the queen's guards ducked into the room. Policemen from nearly every room pounced on the revolutionaries. Several shots were fired. All four revolutionaries were shot. Po was the only one to survive.

The evening before...

Hideki made a surprise visit to see his old friend Maili. Maka was quite suspicious of Hideki, yet he allowed Hideki in the room with the queen's permission.

Maili was still extremely sore from her stitches but attempted to scoot up the bed. "Hideki, what a pleasant surprise! Lizzy and I were just talking about you the other day."

Hideki looked at Maka and then back to the queen, asking, "Is it safe to speak freely, Your Majesty?"

"Hideki, I trust my guards with my life. Please tell me what is bothering you."

Hideki looked at the twins and smiled, and then his smile left as he looked back at Maili and said, "You are in grave danger, Maili. There will be an assassination attempt on your life at any moment. An associate of mine overheard Po and several communists making plans to come to the hospital to assassinate you, the prince, and your twins!"

Maili covered her mouth and looked at Maka. "Are you sure?"

"Yes. Please move rooms and maximize your security immediately. I will leave you with your plans. I would not delay. I wish our visit had had happier circumstances." Hideki turned and left the room.

Maka asked, "Do you trust him, My Queen?" She nodded yes.

Maka got on the phone and told Izzy about the situation. Izzy said, "We would be right over. Lock the door until we get there."

Within the hour, a plan was hatched to trap the revolutionaries, using Austen as bait.

After the shootout, the police handcuffed the wounded Po and walked him over to the queen's new room. "Here is the only survivor, Your Majesty." Po was bleeding and moaning.

Maili just shook her head and cried, "Take him away."

Chapter 14 - The Queen's Hospital Horror

Queen's Hospital, Honolulu, September 16, 1920

Po San was handcuffed to a hospital bed just a few doors down from the queen and her twins. His bullet wounds to the leg, shoulder, and side were not life-threatening. However, the wounds left him low on blood and energy.

Surrounding him were three men. Police Chief Todd Piper began the questioning by saying, "Listen, Mr. San, cooperating is the wisest thing you can do today. We have provided an attorney for your protection, but we have several witnesses there. We have your gun. We have your fingerprints on your gun. We all know you were there because you were shot. We have a witness stating you were planning this. That means it was premeditated, which could get you the death penalty."

Po's attorney spoke, "Under these overwhelming circumstances, Po, I suggest you cooperate with Chief Piper and confess everything you know. Perhaps the judge will go easy on you."

Izzy was also in the back of the room, taking notes.

Po began to speak and managed to get on his soapbox. "I hate what Queen Lydia did to my sister and my parents. I hate how the rich take advantage of the working class. I hate capitalism, and I mistakenly took it out on Maili. However, I do not regret my actions. I hope more people like me take action, as Mao would want. The capitalistic system needs to be destroyed, and we need to start over."

Attorney Jamie Buckkel asked, "Do you think your actions made a difference, Po? Three men are dead, and you are going to spend the rest of your life in prison."

"Do you think I am the only one on this island who wants this? Communism is everywhere now. The *Commission* will see to that. The Russian Revolution was just the beginning. We will take over the press, your education system, Hollywood, your businesses, and eventually your governments."

Buckkel said, "That's rather a bold prediction."

"I would like to tell you who else is going to attempt to take over the throne. I only tell you this because Maili was my childhood friend. If she abdicates, she and her children will be safe. Czar Nicholas should have left Russia. He was a fool and stayed until it was too late."

Izzy asked, "Gentlemen, can we take a short break? Nature calls."

At the front desk, two male nurses appeared for their night shift. "Aloha, gentlemen. How can I help you?" the lady at the front desk asked.

"We are temporary transfers from Haleiwa General. Where do new nurses check in?"

"Oh my, thank goodness. We are so short-staffed. Proceed down the hallway to the first door on the left. You can sign in there."

The two nurses turned left and saw several police officers on duty. They entered the nurse's staff room. A minute later, the new nurses pushed their cart into Po's room.

Po looked at the first man, and his eyes opened wide in fear. "HIRO! NO!"

Hiro pulled out his revolver, shot Po three times, and ran out of the room. They sprinted down the hallway and were gone in seconds.

Chief Piper ran through the door, yelling, "We need a doctor!"

Izzy was still in the restroom when he heard the shots.

Sommy and Tatu heard faint shots close by and ran to the door to lock it. They drew their weapons and barricaded the door.

The police ran after the nurses, but they had disappeared into the night.

Maili screamed, "SOMMY! Protect the twins!"

Attorney Buckkel was in shock. He had never seen anyone shot before. It was so close. His ears were still ringing. He stared at Po's lifeless body. Blood splattered his clothes and notes. "Chief Piper knew those men. He called one Hiro."

Within minutes, Honolulu's chief investigator appeared at the hospital. Inspector Sennot asked Chief Piper, "What do you have for me, Chief?"

Todd still had blood drops on his face. "Two Japanese male nurses; they were both approximately 30; one went by Hiro. They used a revolver. Three shots were fired at close range."

"Where were you when it happened?"

"I was sitting there with my back to the door. I saw the nurse's uniforms out of the corner of my eye and didn't think twice about it. When Po yelled, I turned. I saw their faces for a second, and then I ducked when they fired. Reflexes, I guess. I fell to the ground and grabbed my gun, but they were gone by the time I could aim."

Inspector Sennot thought for a moment: "It was a hit by the mob. Someone didn't want Po to confess. You said they were Japanese?"

In Maili's room, Izzy assured the queen everything was okay. Izzy approached the queen and said, "I am so sorry, Your Majesty. We will have a double police presence outside your door and around the hospital grounds. I am afraid to tell you that Po was murdered."

"Oh, my God. By who?" Maili asked.

"They were Japanese men posing as nurses. One of their names was Hiro."

There was a knock at the door, and a doctor and nurse entered the room. All of the guards drew their guns.

Old Doctor Lau put his hands up, along with Nurse Sara. "Please don't shoot!"

Maili screamed, "It is ok. Doctor Lau has been taking care of me!"

Sara looked down, embarrassed, and said, "I think I need to go change my pants."

Maili apologized as she was leaving: "I am sorry, Sara, Doctor Lau; we are all a little edgy."

Izzy asked Doctor Lau, "Can we get the queen back to the palace? This hospital is not safe."

"She will need constant supervision, and I will make daily checks on her progress. Let me check your stitches, Your Majesty." The doctor looked with approval. "So far, so good. Have you gone to the bathroom yet?"

Embarrassed, she said, "No, Doctor Lau. I haven't eaten in days. I am starving. When can I eat?"

"Izzy, let's get some more fluids in her, and we can sneak an ambulance over to the palace after midnight. Will that work?"

Izzy nodded.

Maili began to cry, "Why does this keep happening to us? We never attack anyone!"

Izzy sat next to the queen and held her hand. "My queen, unfortunately, there is an abundance of evil in this world. Hawaii is heaven, and evil people are envious. We must be even more resolute to protect our kingdom from falling into evil hands. I promise you, we will do everything we can to help you protect it."

Chapter 15 - Momma Bear

Iolani Palace, September 15, 1920.

Sommy pushed Maili in a wheelchair into the cabinet meeting room. Maili was wearing a moo moo instead of her traditional garb. It was still too painful for Maili to walk or dress. Maili was desperate to meet with the cabinet and go on the offensive.

The cabinet greeted the queen with an "Aloha."

"Gentlemen," Maili read over the police report and, in anger, crushed it. She began looking around the room at her trusted advisors. They were all listening attentively. She could see the tops of their ornate chairs, made by a talented carpenter. There were paintings on the walls from past

Kamehamehas and Queen Lydia. Maili knew her monarchy was about to change. "I have thought about this for many, many hours. I believe it is time we are no longer passive with revolutionaries on our islands. These assassination attempts must stop. The first attempt was from American businessmen toward our good King David. Then the Japanese attacked our beloved Queen Lydia. Now Communist China's attack against me shows it may never end. I have some proposals, but I would like to hear your ideas."

Kenneth Doel was in his 70s. He was rather thin. He moved slowly. However, he was still sharp and articulate. He had been a well-respected advisor to the monarchy for several decades. "Your Majesty, I believe that we need to create a secret police force that can spy on these groups. The Americans have the FBI. Perhaps we can send a team to study their technique. We do not want to destroy our trust with the innocent people of Hawaii, but as queen, you should have the right to remove and prevent future terrorist attacks."

Ryan Schildmeyer was the economic advisor. "We have been fortunate, My Queen. If you look around the world these past years- the American President McKinley, the Austrian Archduke Franz Ferdinand, and the Russian Czar Nicholas were all killed by anarchists and communists. It is time we make you and Hawaii safe."

Maili grimaced. "I concur."

Prince Austen spoke up: "Your Majesty, we must arm ourselves for your protection and the defense of all of the Hawaiian islands."

Maili looked up at the ceiling in pain and said, "Weapons, weapons, weapons. That is always your answer. Prince Austen, I have a very special assignment for you. I decree that you will now be our military ambassador to Great Britain. Negotiate all the weapons you believe are necessary within our budget. There is a British ship leaving Pearl Harbor tomorrow. You need to be on it. It goes to Australia and then to Great Britain."

In shock, Austen asked, "But, Your Majesty, what about the twins?"

"Don't you worry, Austen, about the twins. I will take care of them." The cabinet looked around, stunned and murmuring.

"Your Majesty, may I have a word in private?" Austen asked.

"Prince Austen! I think I made myself clear. You are to be on that ship tomorrow and negotiate weapons for Hawaii. Now, Commander Abee, do you have any recommendations to defend the islands?"

Kristofer Abee had been promoted to command all of the Hawaiian forces. Abee came to Hawaii as a child on holiday from England. His parents fell in love with the islands, and he never left. He stroked his thick beard as he spoke. He had worked with Roosevelt during the American President's past visit on how to improve Pearl Harbor and create defense positions for all of the islands. "Your Majesty, we have mobile artillery posted around every island. Our navy has remained small, but I am confident that Roosevelt will help should we be attacked."

Maili painfully smiled with approval. "Mr. Piper, as Police Chief, I expect your officers will be able to listen in on phone calls with probable cause. I would suggest undercover agents in local restaurants where most of the planning has occurred. I would have liked Po San to be interrogated, but I guess our police couldn't protect him from his own terrorists." Maili gave Piper a scolding look. "I want to know who he was working with. I assume you and Inspector Sennott will find out and send them all to prison. If found guilty, I believe the death penalty will be justifiable for the ring leader, and it will send a message to future revolutionaries."

Piper responded, "Yes, Your Majesty. It will be done. My sincere apologies about the loss of your childhood friend and our key witness."

Maili adjourned the meeting, saying, "We will meet next week at the same time and place. Aloha,"

"Aloha", the team responded. Sommy pushed Maili quickly out of the room.

Ryan looked at Austen and said, "Wow! Momma Bear appears to have come out of her slumber."

"Ryan, I honestly don't understand where this came from." Austen appeared to be crying. "My daughters… I won't see my daughters for... months." Ryan placed his hand on Austen's shoulder.

Sommy was wheeling Maili back to her bedroom. "May I speak honestly, My Queen?"

Maili looked up at Sommy and said, "Of course, Sommy. I trust you with my life."

"I don't know if I have ever been more proud of you. We need to rid paradise of these evildoers. I think Austen is one of them. I do not trust him. I hope I am not being too bold."

"Sommy, to be honest, I haven't trusted Austen for some time. I believe he is secretly working with England for his benefit. I know he has stockpiled weapons on Lanai. I know he has made deals with Roosevelt, and for your Tommy guns."

"If I may, My Queen, I have tried to eavesdrop on him and have picked up a few inappropriate conversations about weapons. I apologize for not bringing this to your attention earlier, but I thought you were aware of his dealings. Most of the time, he whispers to his partners, "

"It is unfortunate, but I believe I will keep him in England indefinitely." Maili quietly moaned.

Austen knocked on the queen's door and asked, "May I come in?"

 Maili nodded.

"What is going on, Maili?"

Sommy stood up and crossed her arms. "Address her as your queen." Maili did not look at Austen.

"My Queen, why are you sending me away?"

Maili looked up and stared emotionless into Austen's eyes. "I have realized a few things these past few days. Number one; I am no longer just the queen of Hawaii. I am the mother of the heirs to the throne of Hawaii. I must ensure their safety and the longevity of the crown. I will do whatever it takes to protect Hawaii's future. Number two; I need to get rid of evil on this island, both foreign and domestic. Number three; I honestly want you to be happy, Austen. It appears that selling and buying weapons is what makes you happy. Now go to England and obtain weapons for us. I am asking you to do what you do best—just out in the open."

"When will I get to return?" Austen pleaded.

"That is to be determined. I will send you a generous budget to live off of. Do the right thing, Austen, if you ever want to return."

"Yes, My Queen." Austen bowed and left the room with tremendous sadness.

Sommy turned towards Maili and gave her a high five.

Chapter 16 - Kilauea

Mauna Iki, The Big Island, August 1920

Christopher and Nicholas Lou had dedicated 25 years of their lives to studying the Hawaiian volcanoes. They were also the first to take telescopes up to Mauna Loa to observe the cosmos.

The two volcanologists-turned-amateur astronomers made detailed calculations on the farthest planets, Uranus and Neptune. Christopher was also the first astronomer to discover the return of Halley's comet in 1910 on its 76-year orbit. The two brothers had made names for themselves in the scientific world in both volcanology and astronomy.

Unfortunately, they retired and headed back to California before Kilauea's most active eruption between 1919 and 1920, the Mauna Iki flow. Luckily for them, their legacy was present. Their three daughters, Kory, Kally, and Ally, all stayed on the Big Island. They all majored in volcanology and geology.

November 28, 1919, Kilauea Caldera Summit

Kory Kamaela was standing on the Caldera Crest, looking down into the flat, dark lava floor covering Kilauea. The caldera is massive. A couple of football fields could fit inside the dome. The lava floor appeared lower than yesterday, Kory thought. She took some notes and yelled at her husband, Kava, "Please grab Greyson's hand. He is getting too close to the edge!"

Kava was chasing Greyson and shouted back, "This kid is getting too fast. I think it is too dangerous to bring him on your next visit."

Kory, Kava, and Greyson maneuvered through the dangerous and uneven lava flows until they reached camp. An unsuspecting hiker or child could fall several feet into a crevasse, seriously injuring themselves or even dying. The lava fields are dangerous for many reasons. Often, the molten rock is twisted like taffy in a machine. It remains in peculiar shape as it cools. When the pieces break off, they can be razor sharp. Sometimes a lava tube, which is hollow, could be directly under a hiker, and one could fall several feet to their death with no warning.

Kory waved to get Kally's attention. Kally was playing with her young daughter, Emmy Jo. "Kally, where's Ally?"

"She took Ellie May and Walker with Tevita to explore a lava tube. Do you need me to get them?"

"We need to go observe the caldera floor. Something amazing is happening!" Kory shouted from across the lava field.

"Watch Emmy Jo, and I'll run and fetch her." Kally shouted back.

It gets dark quickly out in the lava fields. The black rock absorbs the light of dusk, and it is impossible to see more than a few feet without moonlight or a lantern. Kory and her sisters decided to stay at camp. She asked the girls to go with her at daybreak.

The next morning, after an early rain, the three scientists were standing on the edge of the caldera as the morning rain turned to steam on the black lava rocks cooked by the blistering morning sun. "OH, MY GOD!" Kory exclaimed, "Look at the floor! I have never seen anything like this!"

Ally shaded her eyes from the glaring sun and said, "It looks so different."

Kory pointed to a pyramid-shaped rock across the volcano and said, "That rock was where the floor was yesterday."

Kally looked at Kory, saying, "That's impossible! That is a hundred feet above the floor. How could the floor have dropped a hundred feet without massive earthquakes? Did any of you feel any tremors last night?"

Ally yawned. "The kids kept me up half the night, and I didn't feel a thing."

The following morning, the floor dropped another hundred feet. Kory looked at her sisters and said,

"This is bad! I think Pele is awakening. We need to move camp and get the kids out of here."

The next day, a small fissure opened south of the caldera. Molten orange lava began oozing out of it. Within days, the caldera floor melted, and bubbling lava rose back up an incredible 300 feet, flowing over the rim. For the next few months, the lava flow ran as fast and wide as a small river for miles until it reached the mighty Pacific. The Mauna Iki, or little mountain flow, would last until August 1920.

August 20, 1920

My dear Queen Maili,

It appears Pele has become tired. After several months of flowing, the caldera at Kilauea appears quiet. There is even better news than that.

The lava flows of Kilauea stretched down to the ocean over four miles from the caldera. These flows added hundreds of acres of new land to the southeastern tip of the Big Island. Your kingdom is growing, my queen!

This past year has given us so much information on the nature of volcanic activity. My sisters and I cannot thank you enough for the opportunity to live and study here on the Big Island.

If it is convenient for you, we would love to visit you and explain what we have learned.

I understand congratulations are in order. I was told you were expecting twins.

With the utmost regard,

Kory Hakulani

University of Stanford

Volcanology Department

Hilo Outreach Satellite

Chapter 17 - Children and Craters

Diamond Head, Oahu, November 20, 1925

It probably wasn't the smartest idea to take small children up to the summit of Diamond Head, Maili thought, but the official royal photographer thought it would be a great chance for some amazing family photographs.

A pleasant rain had fallen in the Honolulu area over the last few days, which sprung the grasses to life. A vibrant green blanketed the inside of the Diamond Head Crater. The tropical sun dried the dirt switchbacks, which made the steep climb doable for people of most ages.

Maili was holding Bethany and Elizabeth's hands. They stopped and looked up to the top.

"Mother, how much further?" Bethany's little legs were doing their best to keep up.

Maili loved her sweet voice and how bright her emerald-green eyes were. "Little Princess, can you see the top of the mountain there?"

Bethany shaded her eyes from the blaring sun. "WOW! Mother, that's a long way to go. Do we have to keep going?"

Elizabeth looked at Bethany and said, "You are such a baby. If I can do it, you can do it." She stuck out her tongue.

Maili scolded Elizabeth, "Now now, girls. We must be supportive of each other. One day, you will both be queens. You must always trust each other, be kind to each other, and support each other. Do you understand?"

"Yes, my queen," Elizabeth said.

"Being a princess is hard." Bethany whined.

Lizzy and Emily, who had been trailing, finally caught up. "Wow! What a beautiful day! Is everyone doing okay?"

Elizabeth said, "Yes, unfortunately, Bethany is complaining again."

Bethany shot back, "I am not."

Maili raised her voice, "Girls! What did I just tell you?"

"Sorry, Mother. Hey, Elizabeth, do you want to hold hands?" Bethany asked.

"Sure I do." Elizabeth let go of Maili's hand as the two swung their hands back and forth.

Lizzy, a few months pregnant, had been holding up the rear. She chided, "Stay on the trail, girls."

Maili rubbed Lizzy's back as she passed by. "How is the Palace Chamberlain feeling today?"

"Extra tired, my queen. I will need water soon. I don't remember it being so steep."

"Where are the rest of the kids?"

"Kenny is way up there with Izzy. Charlie is getting a piggyback ride from Maka, and James is in his papoose with Savita. Why didn't Sommy come?"

"Elizabeth Doel, do you think Sommy is built for this climb? She is as strong as a bull, but not built like a mountain goat." Lizzy chuckled.

Climbing ahead of the royal party were Kory, Kally, and Ally. They also brought their families for photographs and a geology lesson to be shared with the royal family.

The party had gotten an early start, so it wasn't too hot at the summit. There was a small platform where everyone fit, but it was a tight squeeze.

"The view from the top of Diamond Head is unbelievably majestic," Maili thought. To the northwest, the view was of bustling Honolulu and Waikiki Beach. Through the humid air, they could barely make out Pearl Harbor.

"What an amazing backdrop for a royal picture," the photographer said.

The group paused to look out.

The view to the northeast was of the Manoa Valley. The green slopes gently grew until they reached their sharp peaks. Rain clouds floated over the summit, dumping what was left of their moisture. This created a multitude of rainbows all over the valley.

The view to the southeast revealed Koko Head, and off in the distance was Molokai.

Possibly the most amazing view was looking southwest. The mighty blue Pacific extended as far as the eye could see until the ocean met the sky.

Thousands of tiny white caps came and went as the ocean breeze and the ocean waves briefly battled.

Kory began to teach her lesson: "Your Majesty, years ago, my father Christopher and Uncle Nicholas made a hypothesis when they first toured the islands with your good auntie Lydia. They hypothesized that the Hawaiian Islands are moving at a very slow rate north by northwest."

Maili asked, "That is a bold hypothesis. What is your proof?"

"Your Majesty, we are standing on it. As you can see, this volcano, when it was active, blew away to the southeast. Just like at Hanauma Bay, Molokini Crater, Niihau, and now Kileaua. What all of these volcanoes have in common is that they blew up in the same direction."

Ryan Schildmeyer was holding onto Charlie and pointed, "Look, Charlie, there's a whale out in the water!" Everyone looked as Ryan went on, "I think I see your point, professor. It would make sense that as the island moves in one direction, the slower-moving part of the island creates a crack as it pulls away from the rest of the island, allowing the pressure to be released all in the same direction." Everyone looked at Ryan with surprise.

"Precisely, Mr. Schildmeyer. Thank goodness it happened many years ago. I fear Haleakala will also one day do the same, and yes, even Kileaua."

Maili wondered, "What could be the timeline for Haleakala? I think the people of Maui would need a warning."

Kally interjected, "Oh, there should be plenty of warning, Your Majesty. We call Haleakala a dormant, or sleeping, volcano. Thank goodness Diamond Head is extinct. We hypothesize that all the activity here is done. However, when Pele is ready, she and Haleakala will wake up again. It will start with a few small earthquakes. We assume they will become more regular, and then the mountain will become deformed by the pressure below. Lava may or may not be ejected from the summit. Then eventually Maui will shift just enough to the northwest to pull Haleakala apart, and BOOM!" Kally scared all the children.

Lizzy was so caught up in the lesson that she forgot where she was and whipped out her right breast for Baby James in response to his cry for hunger. Izzy glanced over and covered his eyes. "Oh, dear Lord."

Lizzy asked, "What do you foresee as a time frame?"

Ally was the math expert and responded, "Unfortunately, that is unbearably difficult to project. It could be 100 days or 100 years. Maybe 1,000 years if we are lucky."

Maili smiled and said, "Let's hope for 1,000 years then. I shall have a word with Pele and ask for patience on her part."

After all of the photographs had been taken, the group got hungry and trekked back down to the volcano floor, where they had lunch. It was another spectacular day in Hawaii.

Chapter 18 - School Bells

Punahou Elementary, Honolulu, September 5, 1926

Both Maili and Lizzy were shocked at how fast time seemed to fly. They could vividly remember their first day of school. Now, it was their turn to escort their daughters to their first day of kindergarten.

Just like before, crowds and the press gathered to be part of history. The twins rarely got out of the palace. Queen Maili was rather protective of her two treasures, knowing so many assassination attempts around the world had been attempted and carried out. This was the first time most of Hawaii was able to see the young princesses.

Queen Maili was dressed modernly, and the girls were wearing short, bright blue and green moo moos that matched their eyes. Crowds lined the sidewalk and were applauding, curtsying, and bowing as they passed. As the royals approached, most people stopped. Many of the Hawaiians waiting along the sidewalk were mesmerized by the colors of the princesses' eyes.

Following closely behind, just like when they were children, were Lizzy and Emily. Emily was soaking up the attention.

Bethany looked left and right and asked, "Why are so many people here, Mother?"

"They are here to see the future queens begin their school careers." Maili looked down at Bethany and smiled.

As the royals strolled up to the school, Bethany asked, "Mother, I was wondering, where did you get your name?"

"Your grandfather Thomas named me that. He said I may be small, like Hawaii, but I would need to be as strong as rock. Hawaiian culture would be as strong as mine. That's why you need to be strong. For the future of Hawaii."

Elizabeth pushed her bangs out of her eyes. "How did we get our names?"

"I named you Princess Elizabeth after Miss Lizzy, my dearest friend, and you Princess Bethany after your father's mother."

Maili stopped at the entrance gate. She knelt and looked the girls in the eyes. "Now listen, girls. I am going to tell you what my auntie, Queen Lydia, told me on the first day of school."

"What was that, My Queen?" Elizabeth asked.

"She said, "Be strong, be brave, and be kind. Can you do all those things, my princesses?"

"Yes, Mother". "Yes, My Queen." The girls replied.

Approaching the two princesses and Emily was the lovely Madame Robb, who said, "Aloha, Your Majesty, has it really been thirty years?" She curtsied.

Maili asked, "We were so excited when we saw you were the girl's teacher. May I hug you?"

"Oh dear, yes, of course." They embraced and looked at each other.

"Madame Robb, you haven't changed a bit." Madame blushed.

Oh, stop. Can you believe I am 55?" Madame spoke as she blushed.

"That is hard to believe. Wow, this truly takes me back." Maili said.

Elizabeth pulled on Maili's dress and said, "Uh, hmmm."

"Oh, my goodness. Madame Robb, here are my two daughters: Princess Elizabeth and Princess Bethany." Just like their mother thirty years prior, the girls were infatuated with Madame Robb's bright blue eyes.

"Wooooow, your eyes are bright blue like Elizabeth's," Bethany said.

Madame looked at the girls and said, "And my, what beautiful eyes you both have!"

Suddenly another child jumped into the group and said, "My eyes are blue too. I am Emily Schildmeyer. I am the princess's best friend."

Madame Robb stood up and said, "Oh dear, I just had the most amazing déjà vu." Madame finally noticed Lizzy. "Elizabeth Doel?"

Yes, ma'am, it is me. Queen Maili and I are still friends after all these years, and our girls are only a few months apart."

"Well, I can't wait until parent conferences." Madame got the girl's attention by saying, "Let's go, girls." Madame Robb's attention went back to the sidewalk. Madame Robb was standing just inches from a large wahine and looking straight into the large woman's chest. She slowly looked up until she saw the lady's face. It was Sommy. "Umm, Aloha." Madame Robb said:

The school bell rang.

"Aloha, Madame Robb. I am Sommy. I am their bodyguard."

Madame looked at Maili as she smiled and said, "She's our favorite."

The three girls were always the center of attention on the playground. The kindergarteners invented a playground game to see how many times they could catch a glimpse of the twin's eyes. Most of the schoolchildren had never met royalty before. Emily pretended to be their bodyguard, which amused Sommy.

Elizabeth was a natural leader but very emotional. Bethany was logical and empathic. Emily was their spokesperson. The three made a great team.

Lizzy and Maili greeted many parents as they were making their way to and from school. After entering their vehicle, driven by Savita, the young mothers cried and giggled.

"Is the queen okay?" Savita asked as he looked in the rearview mirror.

"Oh, Savita, mothers are very emotional on their child's first day of school."

Lizzy knew this might be a touchy subject, but she asked anyway, "Your Majesty, I was reading in *The Honolulu Times* and started thinking, What is your opinion on *the Scopes Monkey Trial*?"

Well, Lizzy, "I have found that the truth is often a little bit of both arguments. However, in this case, most people believe we are creatures from God, not monkeys. Could it be true that both have happened?"

"I am not sure. I believe that humans are divine. We have souls, and God had a hand in our creation."

"Is it possible that God had a hand in the creation of all creatures?" Maili asked.

"Oh, I believe life is a miracle; there is no doubt about that. I suppose it isn't harmful to teach both

133

in schools. Five plus two equals seven, but so does three plus four." Lizzy quipped.

"Hmmm, Lizzy, that is brilliant."

Chapter 19 - The Flights That Changed Hawaii

San Pablo Bay, California, August 31, 1925

It had only been two decades since Orville and Wilbur Wright flew a 'lighter-than-air' craft in Kittyhawk, North Carolina. The decade of the 20s showcased daredevils in many activities, especially flight. Daring, long-distance air flights became a tempting challenge that would cost many men and women their lives.

On this day, the fog had cleared in San Francisco Bay, and it appeared two naval flying boats would be on their way to Maui. They would be the first non-stop flights from California to Hawaii. Should non-stop flights become a regular event, Hawaii would be forever changed.

Izzy approached the queen, who was chatting with Ryan Schildmeyer about some good economic news: "Your Majesty, the two airplanes have left San Francisco and passed through the Golden Gates. They expect to be here tomorrow night."

Oh, Izzy, that is great news. I would love to dine with the pilot and crew. Can you arrange that?" Maili had one of the twin's model airplanes and was pretending to fly it around like a child.

"I will see to it that we meet with them after they shower and get cleaned up."

"Oh, yes, that is a grand idea."

Commander John Rodgers and his naval crew of five were to be the first to cross the Pacific from California to Hawaii. Their PN-P No. 1 and No. 2 flying boats were pontoon airplanes. The pontoon planes were not extremely aerodynamic, but their design allowed for emergency landings anywhere in the ocean.

The planes had been loaded to the maximum takeoff weight with fuel. Both planes had made attempts to take off in San Francisco Bay but were too heavy. This attempt used several gallons of precious fuel. Both crews decided to dump their heavy parachutes and non-essential equipment into the bay.

On the second attempt, both aircraft became airborne and flew through the Golden Gates westward to Hawaii. The crafts were so heavy that it took more than an hour for them to reach 300 feet in elevation. After two hours, low oil pressure in an engine of PN-9 No. 2 forced it to return.

Eventually, PN-9 No. 1 would reach speeds over 80 knots and climb 1,000 feet into the sunset, headed for Maui.

Izzy returned to the queen and said, "Your Majesty, one plane has had to turn back, but plane No. 1 is on its way."

Maili thought for a moment, "Please inform Commander Lewiston to alert all Hawaiian naval vessels to be ready to assist them tomorrow morning."

"Yes, My Queen." Izzy bowed and left the room.

In the morning, several US and Hawaiian vessels made their way east of all of the islands in preparation for a possible rescue. Commander Rodgers was running low on fuel when he flew over his first refueling vessel. Rodgers should have landed and refueled; however, Commander Rodgers had miscalculated his distance and amount of remaining fuel and unfortunately decided to make a straight shot.

A few hours later, PN-9 No. 1 was lost and running out of fuel somewhere north of Maui. At 5 PM, as the sun was low in the sky, unpredicted head winds put an end to the non-stop flight. Even though radio contact had been made, No. 1 went down in large swells.

Sommy approached the queen at dinner and said, "Your Majesty, I have sad news."

Maili looked up and waited.

"The airplane went down somewhere north of Maui." Sommy shrugged her shoulders as a sign that it didn't look good.

"Please ask Commander Lewiston to come see me immediately."

"Yes, My Queen."

Several days passed. Radio communication had been reached with No. 1, but it could not be found. The fortitude of the crew of No. 1 was admirable. As food ran out, they decided they needed to continue on course. They brilliantly rigged a sail. This pushed them west for several days. They were a few miles north of Kauai when crewmen from a submarine spotted them. A rainstorm gave them plenty of water, but they had lost plenty of weight after not having food for nearly a week.

They would receive a hero's welcome at Iolani Palace. When Commander Rodgers met Princess Elizabeth, she told him, "I knew you'd be safe. I dreamt you would have a luau with the Queen."

Commander Rodgers smiled and said, "Well, Princess, we all thought for a time we'd never see Hawaii. We are so thankful to be here."

January 11, 1935

Queen Maili would meet one of her heroes. Amelia Earhart was an adventurous and brave woman. An American suffragette, Amelia pushed for women's rights around the world. She would dine with Queen Maili right before her maiden solo flight from Honolulu to Oakland.

"Miss Earhart," the queen said.

"Please call me Amelia, Your Majesty."

"Amelia, I am a huge fan. I am so proud of your endeavors and fight for women's rights. My dear Auntie Lydia fought years ago for women's rights. I am hopeful that one day all women will have the right to vote."

"Your Majesty, it is my calling. I use flights as a way to keep the press interested in my voyages. Perhaps I can encourage other girls to become pilots, politicians, or whatever they dream to be," Amelia said.

Maili asked, "Aren't you afraid? This is such a long flight, and you're all by yourself."

"I do get fearful at times. When I am flying into a storm and I cannot see, I have to fly by the instruments. I have to trust that they work perfectly. I have no one up there to help me. It can be exhilarating and frightful at the same time."

Maili smiled and said, "I am glad C & H Sugar could help finance your flight. Is there anything else Hawaii can do for you before you take off?"

"I don't suppose you could grant me a great tailwind, Your Majesty." Amelia smiled at the queen, "but perhaps a large cup of coffee to take with me on the flight would be wonderful."

"I will see what I can do." The queen said it with a smile.

The two powerful and highly respected women hugged. Amelia was headed to Wheeler Field to begin the first solo flight from Hawaii to California.

"Oh, Your Majesty," Amelia remembered, "I am planning an 'around the world flight' in a year or so and would love to have dinner again."

"I would like that too, Amelia. Aloha." Maili waved farewell.

Amelia arrived at Wheeler Field. It was overcast, and a slight drizzle fell on the tarmac. Her chief mechanic, Johnny Tongy, shook her hand and said, "Miss Earhart, all the modifications have been made. The passenger seat has been removed, and another 50-gallon fuel tank was installed."

"I believe if we don't have a strong head wind, that will get us there, Johnny." Amelia boasted.

"We also installed the best two-way radio available. You should be able to communicate with us and Oakland the entire way."

With thousands of fans watching, Amelia took off in her Lockheed 5C Vega.

By the next day, Amelia had flown over the partially completed Golden Gate Bridge and landed at Oakland Airport. Tens of thousands of onlookers were there to witness history. Eleanor Roosevelt invited Amelia to the White House to thank her for advancing women's rights.

Chapter 20 - Nightmares

Iolani Palace, October 28, 1929

Bethany's emerald eyes popped wide open. She gasped for air and sat up in bed. "MOTHER!" she screamed.

Elizabeth looked at her sister through her bright blue eyes and screamed, "Mom!"

Sommy busted through the door. "What is the matter, girls?" She could see that both of them were under tremendous stress. She ran to their bedsides and held them.

Queen Maili was having breakfast when she heard the screams. Maili bolted up the stairs and ran into the princess's bedroom. Noticing the frightened girls in Sommy's arms, she tried to calm them. Maili sat on the bed and asked in a calm voice, "What is the matter with my two beauties?"

Between lip quivers, Bethany said, "I had a horrible dream."

Elizabeth said, "I had one too."

Maili allowed them to relax in Sommy's arms. "Bethany, why don't you start?"

Bethany looked up at Sommy for confirmation, and she nodded.

"Mother, a very scary whale made of smoke was floating over my bed!" Sommy looked at Maili with big, frightened eyes and mouthed "Hina"! Bethany continued, "The smoke lady had fiery red eyes and said the night was approaching! The great sadness was approaching, and then money started to catch fire all around her. She pointed at me and hissed, 'Your eyes!' I could feel the heat, Mother. She grabbed my hand and screamed, but she burned my hand! Look!"

Her palm was red. She buried her face in Sommy's side. Sommy looked at Maili with great concern. Maili inspected her palm. It appeared as if it had been scalded with hot water. Maili softly kissed her palm.

Maili looked at Sommy with concern and then asked Elizabeth, "What did you dream about, Sweetheart?"

"Momma, a ghost man rose from the floor. He was chanting old Hawaiian. He was wearing a tiki mask! Flames were coming out of his eyes and ears. He wore a necklace of a glowing skull around his neck, and he pulled it off in anger and shook it at me! He said death was coming! The underworld will soon be filled with souls. He also said to me, 'Your eyes! Be prepared'."

Maili looked at Sommy again, and she mouthed, "Milu!"

"Well, kaikamahines, they were only dreams." Maili tried to console them.

Bethany looked back at her mother and said, "But it was so real!"

Sommy stood up and got the girls dressed. "A good breakfast will make you feel better. How about some flapjacks and coconut syrup?"

"Oh, that sounds delightful." Elizabeth began to smile.

The twins put on their moo-moos and entered the dining room. Waiting for them was their favorite breakfast, flapjacks, and fruit.

Maili pulled Sommy out of the room and said, "I know of Hina and Milu, but I don't understand the significance."

"Your Majesty, Hina nui te po, is the 'Great Wahine of the Night'. She brings horrible tidings. I fear the girls may witness something tragic with money or war."

"What about Milu? I thought he was the god of the underworld."

"Oh, he is. That was a warning of terrible things to come, Your Majesty. He said the underworld would soon be filled with souls. I imagine war is on the horizon."

October 29, 1929

Maili met with Ryan Schildmeyer. Lizzy popped in with tea and cookies. Maili asked, "Why is Germany at the center of this depression in Europe?"

Ryan grabbed a macadamia nut cookie and nibbled on it. He cleared his throat and began, "Your Majesty, Germany never recovered economically from World War I. Germany took the blame in the Treaty of Versailles, and they were forced to pay other European nations reparations. The Germans were also forced to give up the Rhineland, their best farmland. This further exacerbated their economic problems."

The queen was curious: "Why has it taken so long to recover?"

"Riots and political strife motivated the Weimar Republic to print money to pay off its debt, causing severe inflation. A loaf of bread cost over a million marks!"

"We need to prevent inflation," Maili warned. "I know that our dollars are backed by gold."

Ryan held Lizzy's hand and smiled. "That is how it is supposed to work. The United States tried to assist the Germans. They loaned the Weimar Republic millions of dollars, but it wasn't enough. A horrible economic depression impacted the Germans. The world learned we were all connected, and the financial house of cards is crumbling."

"Please advise me on how we can protect our economy," Maili asked Ryan.

"We may need a deflationary practice or lower prices of sugar, pineapple, and coffee to temporarily offset the lowered demand."

Lizzy asked, "Is there a possibility of another coup?"

Ryan leaned back in his chair and looked up with sadness. "Discontent opened the door for a new political party in Germany called the NAZIS, the Nationalist German Workers Party. Like Mussolini in Italy, fascism is on the rise. So too is violence."

Izzy came in with the daily newspaper and said, "More bad news, Your Majesty. The NY Stock Market crashed!"

Ryan placed his forehead in his hands and pulled his hair back. "This is what I was afraid of, Your Majesty. Trouble in Europe and a slowdown in the American economy have come to a head. When panic hits the stock market, stock prices plummet. Many people lost their fortunes today. Thousands of people ran to banks to get any cash that was left.

These 'bank runs' will be the true beginning of a great economic slowdown."

"How do you know this, Ryan?" Lizzy wondered why.

"It is truly horrible news, but not what most people think. Most people don't own stocks. However, things like this create panic. The bank runs are the worst."

Maili asked, "What is a bank run?"

"When people fear their money will be gone, they run to the bank to clean out their savings. When a bank runs out of cash, it closes. This freezes out the majority of those who save there. Most of the deposits are loaned out to people. The money is not in the bank vault. Then people stop spending. People won't want to spend their last $20 on a meal, so restaurants will close. Then there will be thousands of layoffs for their employees. Business after business will close their doors."

"What can we do to prevent this from happening here?" Maili became quite concerned.

"Your Majesty, that is the million-dollar question. I would suggest the following: The most important thing is that we must temporarily close the banks. I believe you should go on the radio to assure the people that our banks are secure."

"Won't that create more panic when they reopen?" Maili asked.

"I would state in your emergency radio address that savers can only withdraw 10% of their savings per week. Also, you could guarantee the deposits to remove any future runs. We have plenty of gold in our treasury, My Queen."

Maili looked at Ryan for a moment and said, "This is my first crisis as queen. I need to be positive about this, Ryan. Do you think this will keep the Hawaiians from panicking?"

"I do, Your Majesty. However, tourism will be hit hard. The middle class may scale back their vacations. We might need to advertise in Hollywood and San Francisco to help generate tourism from the wealthy." Ryan explained.

Sommy had been standing by the door. "Your Majesty, your girls' nightmares! First, they saw a financial crisis. Now, there is a civil war in China.

There are also rumors of a Japanese invasion of Manchuria. They may have a special gift."

Ryan looked in bewilderment at Lizzy, and she said, "I will tell you later."

Chapter 21- Two puppies

Iolani Palace, November 1, 1929

Maili and Sommy were enjoying breakfast in the dining room. Maili looked at Sommy and said, "I think it's time for," she winked, "you know what."

Sommy's eyes and smile said it all. Sommy exited quickly.

Maili asked Tatu to bring down the girls. "Yes, Queen Maili." Tatu clasped his hands together and left the room.

Sommy peaked around the back entrance of the dining room. She only showed half of her face. She slyly leaned back out of view. Bethany and Elizabeth entered the dining room, and Maili was standing with an awkward look on her face.

Bethany asked, "What is going on, Mother?"

"Girls, I was about your age when Queen Lydia gave me my first taste of responsibility. I think it is time for the two of you to experience the same. Your lives are about to change. Please, you must promise me that you will be patient, caring, and attentive."

"We promise, Mother." The girls said it excitedly.

Maili looked back and raised her voice. "Sommy, bring them in."

Sommy entered the room with her hands behind her back and said, "Close your eyes, princesses."

The twins closed their eyes as they smiled and giggled. Sommy stepped towards the twins and brought her hands forward. Maili began to cry, "Open your eyes, girls."

Fitting into Sommy's large hands were two petite dachshunds. They could not have been much more than two pounds. One female was black and had a puffy patch of hair on her head, and the other female was brown with a black patch around one eye.

The twins screamed and jumped for joy. They both began to blubber as Bethany said, "Oh my goodness. She's perfect." The twins took them from Sommy. They brought them into their chests and squeezed them. Sommy became choked up at the sight.

Maili wiped away her tears and said, "Elizabeth, what are you going to name her?"

Elizabeth stroked her little brown head and thought, "I will name you Jelly, because you are so sweet."

"Bethany, it's your turn."

"Oh, Mother. She's so adorable. I will name her after my favorite little Russian doll, Genny. You are my little Genny."

Maili placed her hand on their shoulders as she leaned in. "In Hawaiian culture, you are not pet owners; you are their 'Kahu'! You are Jelly and Genny's guardians and protectors. It is important that you feed, play, and comfort these little puppies. You need to take them outside on a regular basis so they can relieve themselves. We definitely don't want them going on your bedroom floor."

The puppies were instantly attached to the girls and began licking the twins' faces and wagging their little tails. It was love at first sight.

Jelly and Genny would almost become as popular as the twins. Everywhere they went, the puppies were present, giving laughs and 'awws' everywhere they went.

Chapter 22 - The Ancient Ones

The Princess' Bedroom, October 8, 1934

The ancient ones often visited the twins in their dreams and often passed on stories of the kings of days gone by. Sometimes they wanted something more.

The girls' nightmares also continued throughout their teen years. These nightmares were so intense that Bethany and Elizabeth decided to remain together in their childhood bedroom. It gave them comfort to be near each other.

 Tonight, Bethany was dreaming she was flying over the ocean. She could see Molokai and Maui below as she clutched Genny tightly. She was above the puffy clouds and flying very fast, much faster than a bird, but she could not feel the wind. She flew over Lanai and Kahoolawe across the Alenuihaha Channel. She flew to the southernmost area of the Big Island.

Princess Bethany looked to the horizon. She had never seen it so vast before. She thought, "My, the ocean is so massive." Bethany was wearing a traditional grass skirt, a haku, and a bracelet haku. Her flower lei was made of soft and large plumerias. She grabbed the lei and sniffed it for plumeria, her favorite scent.

Bethany looked down. She was directly over the caldera of Kilauea. It was pitch black at the bottom, and she started to fall. She was falling fast. She began to scream! As she reached just a few feet above the dome, she gently floated to the rough black lava rock. She could feel the sharp edges of lava rocks on her feet. Bethany placed Genny on the caldera floor. She looked in all directions. The cliffs went nearly straight up. "How am I going to get out of here?" She thought.

Twenty feet ahead of her, lava began to glow orange. Genny started to bark ferociously. The lava beneath her bare feet was still black, but it was getting warmer. The orange lava began to bubble. Rising slowly from the caldera floor, there rose a blob of lava, and it grew into the shape of a human. As the shape formed, Bethany could make out a petite Polynesian wahine. The wahine transformed from bright orange lava into a beautiful goddess. Her brilliant red dress shimmered as if it were full of light. Her opal eyes captivated Bethany. Her hair flowed in slow motion, as if she were under water. Genny sat, became calm, and wagged her tail as if she perceived no danger.

"Bethany!" The whale's voice was powerful yet soft. "I am Pele, the goddess of all of Hawaii's volcanoes. I brought you here to warn you. Your sister is in danger. You must protect her."

Bethany could not speak.

"Your emerald eyes tell me you are destined for greatness one day, Princess. However, your fate is not set. Your sister must be careful when she rides! The future of Hawaii will depend on your bravery."

Bethany still could not talk, but Pele could hear her thoughts: "What must I do?"

"Your fate will be revealed in time, my princess." Pele's voice began to gurgle.

Pele's dress and her skin slowly transformed back into black and orange lava. She slowly sank back into the caldera. Within seconds, the caldera floor was just as it appeared when Bethany had landed.

The ancient ones paid Princess Elizabeth a visit as well. Elizabeth began dreaming of rainbows swirling above her bed. They gave her great joy. Jelly jumped up at the rainbow and tried to lick it.

Multiple rainbows began twisting together and grew larger until the entire room became a blur of colors. Elizabeth became irritated that her beautiful rainbow was now a blur. To her right, she heard a strange man's laugh. Then the cackle was to her left. Above her bed floated a long and lean man. His face was three feet long. He had a large, evil grin. His body stretched over half of the room, and his arms were like long, wet noodles wiggling to and fro.

Elizabeth yelled, "Why did you take away my rainbow? I love rainbows!"

The weird man laughed in her face. "Well, I like chaos. I like magic, and you, my dear, are full of it. May I borrow some?"

"You are so strange! Who are you?" Elizabeth commanded

"You, my dear, are not yet strong enough to command me. I will tell you who I am if you allow me to 'borrow' some of your magic," the strange apparition said eerily.

"No deal. Go away, or I'll get Sommy to take care of you." The princess insisted.

The strange man disappeared for a moment. In her sleep, she heard a loud thump.

The ghost appeared again. This time he was just inches from the princess' face. "I have taken care of Sommy. Jelly barked at the entity. Now give me your magic or I will take your dog's life!"

Maka was awake on the first floor and heard a thump. Sommy was at the bottom of the stairs in pain. "Sommy, what happened, Cousin?" Maka ran to her aid.

Sommy was holding her wrist. "This may sound weird, but I was a few steps away from the bottom step, and someone pushed me."

"SOMMY!" The princess screamed!

Maka, in a panic, said, "Stay here, Sommy. Let me check on the princess!" Maka sprinted up the stairs, down the hall, and burst into the twins' room. He turned on the light. Both girls were crying. "WHAT? What is the matter? Did you have another vision?" They shook their heads, yes. "I will be right back. Let me get the queen."

Maka ran down the hall and knocked loudly on the queen's door. "Your Majesty! I am sorry to bother you, but we have an issue with the princesses."

"Ok, I will be right there."

Maka ran back to the girls' room and said, "Your mother will be right here. I need to check on Sommy."

Elizabeth asked, "Did she fall down the stairs?"

Maka raised his eyebrows and asked, "How did you know that?"

Sommy lumbered up the stairs in pain and met the queen in the twins' room. Maili asked, "Not another vision?"

Bethany said, "Mother, I met Pele. She warned me Elizabeth was in trouble. I met her at Kileaua, on the lava dome. Look at my feet."

Maili hustled over to her bedside and inspected her soles. "Oh my God!" They were black and had blisters. "How is this possible? Maka, can we get a doctor here, please?"

"Yes, My Queen." Maka ran out of the room.

"Momma, I had a very, very strange man floating over me. He said he likes chaos, and I have magic." Elizabeth looked puzzled.

Holding her wrist, Sommy groaned, "That is Kanaloa. He is the god of mischief. What did you say when he asked you for your magic?"

"I said no and that I would call for you. That's when he pushed you! I don't like him. He said I would get stronger. He will be back!"

Maili asked Sommy to sit until the doctor came.

Bethany leaned over to Elizabeth and whispered, "Pele warned me about your riding."

Elizabeth shushed her sister.

"If Mother finds out you're still riding that motorcycle instead of horses, she is going to ground you!"

"Well, she's not going to find out now, is she?" Elizabeth glared at her sister.

Maili leaned over to Sommy and asked, "What are those two plotting?" I know those looks.

The next day, Kilauea erupted. It continued for 30 straight days.

Chapter 23 - Beauties and the Boys

Waikiki, October 20, 1934

The royal family had gathered at Waikiki Beach. It was time to take a royal family photograph. Maili, Elizabeth, and Bethany were in formal gowns. The photographer set up a throne on the beach so Diamond Head would be in the background. It was a perfect autumn afternoon. The surf was light. The breeze was too The orange glow from the sun was behind the photographer and lit the family with a heartwarming hue.

Along with the royal family were the Schildmeyers: Ryan, Lizzy, Kenny, Emily, Charlie, James, and nine-year-old Hannah. They were waiting for their turn to join the royal family.

Along the beach, a large group of Hawaiians and tourists gathered to watch the royal family with their dear friends.

Bethany elbowed Elizabeth. "Look, Elizabeth, your 'boyfriend' Taufa has come out to watch the spectacle."

Elizabeth continued to face forward but glanced over quickly with her eyes. "He's not my boyfriend. He wishes he was."

Bethany began to tease, "Should I ask him if he wants to get in the picture?" Elizabeth glared at Bethany.

The photographer yelled, "Smiles, Your Royal Highnesses."

Maili looked at her daughters and, with a fake smile, said, "Will you two stop teasing each other? We are in public." The Schildmeyers joined the royal family for a group photo.

Maka was staring at the queen as he petted Jelly's head. Sommy noticed him staring. "And what, may I ask, are you gaping at?"

Maka sighed, "Oh, the most beautiful wahine in all of Hawaii."

"I thought I was the most beautiful wahine in Hawaii," Sommy teased.

"You are adorable, Sommy, but not my type." Maka punched her arm.

"What's wrong with a six-foot, 250-pound wahine with a cast?" Sommy hit Maka in the chest with it.

"OUCH!" He screamed, getting the family's attention.

Emily leaned over to Bethany and Elizabeth and whispered, "I think someone has a crush on the queen."

"Who?" Bethany whispered back.

"Don't look now, but he's standing next to Sommy." Emily continued to look at the camera.

"MAKA?" Maili looked up at Bethany with a grimace.

"Sorry, Mother." Bethany thought for a moment and whispered, "He does make the googoo eyes at her. And he is pretty handsome."

Lizzy shushed the girls.

The photographer waved over the guards.

Emily said, "This should be interesting."

Sommy, along with Maka, Izzy, Savita, and Tatu, joined the group. The photographer snapped the picture as he said, "Say cheese!" just as a large wave washed up around everyone's feet. The group ran up the beach, laughing. The admirers got a great chuckle watching the royals run from the ocean wave.

Maka ran to the queen and asked, "May I escort, my queen?"

Emily said, "Look. See, I told you." The girls giggled.

Maili's feet were sinking into the beach, and she noticed a small, black pebble amongst the white grains of sand. Maili picked it up and stared at it for a moment. It made her think of her name. She thought back to her father figure, Koa. She missed him so much. She thought, "He's been gone for so many years, and yet I can see his face and hear his voice. I so adored that man."

"My Queen, is everything okay?" Maka snapped Maili out of her daydream.

"Oh. Oh yes, Maka. Mahalo."

As the bodyguards opened up a passage for the two families to make their way to supper, Lizzy noticed Hideki in the crowd.

"Oh, Hideki! It has been so long. Where have you been hiding?"

Maili approached her two old friends. Hideki bowed. "Your Majesty, Lizzy, I have many projects I am currently working on. Perhaps I can share them with the two of you one day." Maka stepped in front of Maili.

Bethany grabbed Emily's arm and said, "Did you see that? Maka just cut that kane off that Mother was flirting with."

Elizabeth and Charlie gathered next to the gossiping girls and asked, "What are you two chatting about?"

"Look at Maka. I think he is jealous." The girls giggled again.

"Aloha, Princess. Aloha, Princess", Taufa and Papu shouted.

Emily traipsed over, "Aloha boys." She teased the princesses by pretending to flirt with their male friends.

"Aloha, Taufa," Elizabeth said, smiling. "A hui hou boys," she wiggled her fingers goodbye as she traversed past.

"Aloha, Papu." Bethany also smiled as she strolled by.

Taufa grabbed Papu around the neck and said, "She said Aloha to me! Princess Elizabeth has to be the prettiest girl in the world."

"Nah, Cousin. Bethany has her beat by a mile. Those eyes! She makes my toes sweat."

Maka politely reminded the queen about supper. "Well, Aloha, Hideki. I hope to see you soon." Maka was fuming.

Taufa looked at Papu and said, "Cousin, stop dreaming. Why would beauties like that ever like boys like us?"

Papu bragged, "Well, I am a very handsome kane. You are okay, I guess, Taufa. Maybe you could be her servant one day."

"HA! Very funny, Papu. I am going to join the military. Wahines love a kane in a uniform!" Taufa tugged on his shirt to pull it down straight.

Papu laughed. "I bet you a hundred coconuts you don't ask her to the dance!"

"ONE HUNDRED COCONUTS! It's a bet." They shook hands.

Chapter 24 - Maili Visits the League of Nations

London, England, April 1, 1935

Maili's plane touched down on the tarmac in London, England. The weather was gloomy, but the crowd was electric. The queen's admirers could not have been more exuberant. Waiting with a bouquet was her husband, Austen. It had been years since they had seen each other.

The Queen of Hawaii carefully shuffled down the airplane ramp. She was wearing a bright orange sarong that fit snuggly. Her haku had white plumerias sprinkled with dark green leaves. Austen's heart was racing after his long-awaited glimpse of Maili. He had hoped he might rekindle their relationship.

"Aloha, Your Majesty. It is so great to finally see you." Austen kissed her on both cheeks. He stood back and bowed.

Maili could barely hear as the crowd continued screaming. It was rare for another monarch to visit England, and the British people were excited to see a royal from the other side of the world.

The queen remained regal and calm. "Aloha, Austen. It is nice to see you as well. Is there somewhere we can talk that is not so loud?" Maili's security team was present. Izzy and Tatu led the royal couple through the cheering crowd, while Maka and Sommy stayed by her side.

Austen attempted to interlock arms with the queen, but Maka cut between them. Austen became irritated but did not show it. He yelled at Izzy to make their way to his awaiting vehicle.

Photographers continued to take pictures that flashed so brightly. Maili saw nothing but white spots. The entourage gathered in two cars and rolled up the windows, but the cheering of the crowd could still be heard. "My, the people of London sure are ecstatic to see the Queen of Hawaii." Austen joyfully said:

Sommy laughed a deep laugh and said, "You are right about that, Ol' Chap." Sommy replied, trying to sound British. Austen politely smiled, then directed his attention back to Maili as she waved to her fans.

"Your Majesty, you look ravishing. The fresh Hawaiian air is treating you well."

"Mahalo, Austen. You are looking good too. How is the armor business these days?"

Austen looked oddly at the queen and said, "From our last correspondence, it appears you are receiving plenty of weapons and ammunition. I am currently working on financing and shipping several fighter aircraft to Oahu. The information I have received from Germany and Japan is that the newest airplanes are going to change warfare."

"May I ask you why you address me as 'Your Majesty', and not 'My Queen', like you used to?"

Austen again seemed perplexed. "Maili, it was just a sign of respect."

"I took it as perhaps you have another king or queen now?"

"No, not at all, Maili."

"It appears you have found your happy place here in England. I request that you remain here and continue to increase military trade for our sugar and fruits." Maili said it sternly.

Austen exhaled heavily and looked down. Maili glanced at Sommy, and she had to turn away so as not to laugh.

"Maili, I was hopeful I could return to Hawaii with you. I miss you, Elizabeth, and Bethany so much." Austen continued to look down.

"Austen, if I may ask, If you miss us so much, why don't you write more?" Maili glared at Austen.

"Honestly… I had given up hope of ever seeing my family again. Therefore, I tried to move on. I am a different person now, My Queen. I promise to dedicate myself to you and our daughters."

"Austen, I will need some time to think about us. Perhaps after my trip to the League of Nations, you can come to visit us along with your new airplanes." Maili patted his knee.

"I would like that very much, Your Majesty, I mean, My Queen." Austen took a deep breath. "By the way, King George requested your attendance at dinner tonight. Will you attend?"

Maili looked at Sommy and asked, "Will my guards be able to attend?"

"Oh yes, of course, there is plenty of room at Buckingham Palace." Austen changed his attitude:

"Sommy, you are in for quite a treat. Imagine Iolani Palace times one hundred."

Sommy asked, "Are their chairs large? I need a little extra room." Sommy smiled.

Later that evening...

With much fanfare, the dinner with King George went swimmingly. The two royal families had much to talk about.

As the evening waned, King George and Queen Maili began to stroll along the grand hallways. King George's health was getting worse by the day, and his ability to walk, even with a cane, was difficult. Alongside the pair was Princess Elizabeth, heir to the British throne. Following farther back were Austen and her guards.

The conversation turned serious as the subject of war was addressed. Princess Elizabeth became quite concerned about the military advancement of the Japanese. The princess specifically had concerns about Australia and the disruption of the flow of oil from Indonesia.

Maili looked into Elizabeth's eyes. Elizabeth was star-struck.

"Dear Princess, I assure you that the Americans and my military advisors are quite aware of the Japanese aggression in the Pacific. It wasn't that long ago that they attempted to assassinate Queen Lydia and invade Kauai. We have been getting our military ready in case they attack us again."

With a strong, proper British accent, "Very good, Queen Maili. I hope we can continue our strong relationship for years to come." Elizabeth smiled cordially.

Two days later...

Once again, the Europeans went crazy over the world's newest celebrity. This time it was in Geneva, Switzerland, the headquarters of the League of Nations. Maili was in awe. She had never seen such majestic mountains. The Alps already had a few feet of snow on their peaks. As Maili stepped down onto the tarmac, she stood and stared for minutes at their beauty. She had seen snow on the top of Mauna Loa and Mauna Kea before, but that did not come close to the grandeur of the Swiss Alps.

Several leaders around the world were asked to speak at the League of Nations. The international political body had one main goal: never repeat the mistakes that led to World War I.

Secretary-General Joseph Avenol stood at the podium and said, "Today, we have several special guests. Leaders from around the world are here today to promote peace and push for an economic recovery. Our first guest is Queen Maili Grace Kaanapali Kamaka, 'eha of Hawaii!" The diplomats erupted with applause.

Maili wore a formal, form-fitting black gown with a sash across her chest. She wore her traditional haku with pink and lavender flowers that popped against her golden tan. Her bright white teeth seemed to beam as she smiled. When she blinked, it appeared to be in slow motion. Many male diplomats felt the need to sit down so as not to reveal their true feelings.

"Ladies and gentlemen of the world, I came to you today to bring a message of hope. My hope, like yours, is for a peaceful planet. The citizens of the world should never know the horrors of war again. The Great War ended just 17 years ago. There is a new generation of children who do not know the pain of having their fathers go off to battle and never return or return injured. These children do not know the horrors of having their towns and villages bombed and burned. There is a new generation of young men who may now start their families and watch their children grow up to adulthood. We must continue to negotiate to stop the war at all costs. Some countries, like Japan and Germany, have decided to leave the League of Nations. I implore Chancellor Hitler and Emperor Hirohito to return your diplomats to this body and work steadfastly for peace. I close by begging every member here to speak openly and honestly to keep our world at peace. Mahalo for this time, and ALOOOOO HA!"

The diplomats responded with a heartfelt "ALOOOOO HA!"

Like Neville Chamberlain of England and Edourd Deladier of France, Maili's naivete about the aggressive nature of the fascists only sealed the fate of Europe and later the world.

As the ancestors foretold, Maili would change the world. However, the headlines were not taken so positively by the future Axis Powers.

Chapter 25 - The Twins and Schildmeyers

Honolulu, Oahu, Hawaii, April 3, 1935

Princess Bethany yawned and blinked to get the sleep out of her eyes. She turned toward the sleeping Elizabeth. Elizabeth's mouth was open. Bethany rolled over and reached out her pointer finger, stuck it in Elizabeth's mouth, and shook her face with it.

"WHAT? What the heck are you doing, Bethany, you dumdum?" Elizabeth yelled. "I was finally having a wonderful dream." Genny and Jelly started jumping on Elizabeth's face, trying to wake her up.

She pushed them away. "You shouldn't refer to the Princess of Hawaii as a dumdum, you dummy!" Bethany was laughing at her twin's reaction. "Were you dreaming about Taufa again?"

"You are so weird sometimes. Did you have any bad dreams for you last night?" Elizabeth stretched and yawned.

"Not last night. Hey, I was thinking of calling the cabinet together today. Mother, I mean, the queen is not expected back for a few more days, and we need to practice 'ruling'." Bethany pulled back the drapes to check on the weather. "It looks like another beautiful day in paradise."

"What will we discuss, Princess Dumdum?" Elizabeth smirked.

"Let's talk about it at breakfast. The Schildmeyers are all coming over. They should be here any moment."

Most breakfasts weren't formal at the palace. The princesses liked to enjoy their company, especially if it was with the Schildmeyers. Ryan and Lizzy greeted the twins at the bottom of the stairs of Iolani Palace, and they brought everyone but Kenny. Emily, Hannah, James, and Charlie dressed up for an official breakfast with the princesses.

"Aloha, Princess Bethany. Aloha, Princess Elizabeth," Lizzy and Ryan bowed. The twins curtsied.

"Aloha, Uncle Ryan. Aloha, Auntie Lizzy. Do you see how they addressed me first? That's because I'm the number one princess."

"I guess you are the number one princess, dum dum." Elizabeth greeted the Schildmeyers and proceeded to the dining area, where she began hugging her lifelong friends.

During the meal, there was plenty of chatter. It was always filled with laughter and pleasantries.

Elizabeth asked, "Where's Kenny?"

Lizzy looked down and said, "He's off training somewhere. I have a feeling war is approaching. He keeps talking about Japanese aggression."

Bethany changed the mood of the conversation and asked Ryan, "Elizabeth and I want to call the cabinet together tomorrow to address some issues. Will you gather them for us? We could make it a working lunch."

Ryan cleared his throat and said, "Of course, Princess. What will be on the agenda?"

"Chief Kaanapali from Maui needs assistance with breaker walls in Old La Haina. Chief Puki 'i of the Big Island has concerns about Kiluaea cutting off Hilo again, and Chieftess Ma 'ama of Molokai said she has concerns about their road to Kalaupapa having been destroyed again, making travel by land impossible. Plus, we need to work with the Americans at Pearl."

"Very good, Princess. It will be scheduled. Do you know how the road to Kalaupapa got destroyed?" Ryan asked.

Chieftess Ma'ama claims it was the Menehune causing mischief again."

Ryan excused himself and left the room.

"Auntie Lizzy, do you remember seeing the Menehune when you were rescued?" Bethany asked.

"It was like a dream, my princess. I remember the feeling of flying out of the water and landing on the shore. Then your beautiful mother appeared when she saw the first one. It was so strange. Your mother definitely saw them twice. She snuck out again, caught Queen Lydia and Koa being romantic, and saw another one."

Elizabeth said, "Whaaaaaaat? Our mother snuck out. Just wait until I see her again. She has some answering to do."

Lizzy's eyes got big. "Maybe I should have kept that a secret."

Bethany leaned back and crossed her arms. "Auntie Lydia had an affair with Koa? So that sort of thing does happen. Hmmmm."

Emily giggled.

Lizzy asked with suspicion, "What's going on?"

Bethany placed her napkin over her face so as not to give away her smile. "Oh, nothing, Aunt Lizzy."

The children lingered for hours as the old friends caught up with the latest school events and the crazy dreams the twins continued to experience.

At the end of breakfast, Emily grabbed Elizabeth's arm, and they roamed through the garden together. The girls had some serious boy talk to discuss.

The next day...

The cabinet started the meeting by slowly stepping through the buffet line. The members continued to compliment and thank the twins for the special treat.

Princess Bethany raised her voice to get the cabinet's attention and allowed Elizabeth to start the meeting. The twins discussed before the meeting that they were equal players and needed to present themselves as such in public. For only being 15 years old, the princesses were quite politically savvy.

The items on the itinerary were addressed, and as the meeting was about to close, Walt Underson entered the room.

"Please pardon my lack of punctuality. I had to wait until my kid's plane landed at Hickem. I tried to hurry without speeding, of course. Here is my son, Wally. He is 15. Just like you, princesses. And this is my daughter Gillian; she is 12."

Bethany and Elizabeth raised their eyebrows as Wally strutted in. He was quite tall and muscular. Bethany elbowed Elizabeth. She leaned over to Elizabeth and whispered, "He's cute."

Wally was unsure of the protocol and bowed. The princesses smiled. Wally's face turned red. Gillian had red hair and freckles. She had thick glasses, which helped her reading habit of nearly 8 hours a day.

With a strong lisp, she said, "Aloha, Princess Bethany, and Princess Elizabeth. It is my honor to meet you. I spent the ten-hour flight reading up on Hawaiian history and culture. I have so many questions, if your highness would have some time in the near future, "Gillian asked.

Bethany looked at Elizabeth, trying not to giggle. "I don't see why not. We are almost finished here, and we can chat in just a moment." Bethany smiled at Gillian.

Bethany asked Walt, "Will we have more ships and airplanes to protect our islands, Mr. Underson?"

"Your Majesty, President Roosevelt is a big Navy man and wants to expand America's naval presence all over the Pacific. His goal is to have most of the repairs done here at Pearl Harbor. That will require an increased buildup of personnel. That will bring thousands of men to the islands and cause a boom to the Hawaiian economy."

Bethany looked back at Elizabeth and said, "The queen will be pleased."

The meeting ended on a high note. Elizabeth asked Wally and Gillian, "Would you like a tour of the palace?"

Wally smiled and replied, "That would be wonderful."

"I know just the person. Give me a minute." Elizabeth asked her bodyguard, Kai, if he would find Emily and Charlie and bring them to the meeting room.

The princesses and Wally continued some idle chitchat until Emily showed up.

"Aloha, Princess. How can I help you?" Emily inquired.

Elizabeth sauntered over to Wally and placed her hand on his shoulder. "This is Wally Underson. He is new here in Hawaii and needs a tour of the palace grounds."

Emily looked up at Wally. She stared for a moment and smiled as her cheeks became rose-colored. "This way, Wally." Emily looked back at Elizabeth and mouthed, "Wow".

Charlie appeared. "Yes, my highnesses?"

"Charlie, this is Gillian Underson. Please show her around the palace and meet us back in the sun room for tea and cookies later." Elizabeth ordered.

Elizabeth leaned on Bethany and said, "Ahh, I love playing Cupid. Emily was just telling me this morning how she couldn't find a kane. It was like the gods were listening and answering our prayers."

Chapter 26 - Queen Maili Returns from Europe

Oahu, Hawaii, April 6, 1935.

Queen Maili arrived at Hickem Air Base after a long flight around the world. Thousands of her beloved subjects greeted her with tremendous love and fanfare.

Waiting on the tarmac were her two daughters. Bethany and Elizabeth presented Queen Maili with two floral leis. "Aloha Mother. Aloha Momma. We missed you so much."

Maili lifted the lei to her nose and breathed in slowly and deeply. "Oh, how I missed Hawaii and my daughters."

Bethany curtsied and then hugged her mother, asking, "How is Father?"

Maili looked at Sommy and smiled. "Well, let's say he is anxious to return to Hawaii. He said he misses you greatly."

Elizabeth crossed her arms and asked, "Then why doesn't he write?"

"We addressed that issue, Princess. Your father will visit in a few months, and you can bring that up with him."

This got Maka's attention. He was unaware of the queen's plans. He leaned over to Izzy and asked, "Did you know about this?" Izzy shook his head.

The twins caught Sommy's eye and ran to her. They both jumped on her at the same time, and Sommy caught them both. "Aloha, Princesses. I missed you." Sommy's children ran up to her, and they all hugged.

Izzy looked at Maka and said, "Hey, by the way, was that you that stunk up the lua?"

"Oh no, Cousin," he waved his hand in front of his nose, "that was Sommy!" and they both laughed.

The queen, her daughters, and her entourage approached the line of admirers. Maili waved and smiled. The Hawaiians were enamored as the three royal wahines passed by and touched their hands. Maili suddenly stopped as she caught a glimpse of Hideki. Hideki inched closer to the queen, and Maka recognized him too. Maka swiftly stepped in to block Hideki from getting too close.

Hideki's training and instincts kicked in and blocked Maka's hand as he got into a fighting stance. Seeing this, Izzy jumped into action to defend his colleague. A scuffle ensued. Jelly escaped from Elizabeth's arms and started biting Hideki's ankle. Hideki kicked her off.

The twins screamed and jumped back as Sommy stood in front of the queen. "IZZY! MAKA! It's ok. It's Hideki."

Maili pushed through the crowd and picked up Jelly. "What is going on here?"

Izzy bowed in shame. "Hideki attacked Maka, and I jumped in."

Hideki bowed and said, "A thousand apologies, Your Majesty. I over-reacted."

"Mahalo, gentlemen, it's ok. It's been a long trip, and we are all tired." Maili shook her head and said, "I return home to this? Let's get to Iolani," a frustrated Maili said.

Maka looked back at Hideki and placed his finger in Hideki's face, saying, "Don't ever do that again! I don't care if the queen knows you or not."

Hideki glared into Maka's eyes, not backing down.

Bethany asked, "Mother, why does Hideki keep showing up? He's kind of creepy, plus he kicked Jelly. Didn't he kill your little dog, Coconut?"

"I think he wants to become friends again. I am not sure if I trust him. He didn't really kill Coconut. It was an unfortunate accident."

Elizabeth questioned, "If you don't trust him, Momma, why don't you send some spies out to see if he means the monarchy harm?"

"That's a great idea, Princess. So, how was Hawaii in my absence?"

Bethany was excited to share, "We ran our first cabinet meeting!"

"You did? How did that go?" The royals got into their vehicle.

Bethany leaned in and smooched Maili on the cheek. "It was my idea, but Princess Dum Dum did help."

"Aren't you both too old to be calling each other silly names?"

"I suppose so, Mother, but it is fun." Bethany stuck her thumbs in her ears and wiggled her fingers.

Elizabeth jumped in, saying, "Well, I set up Emily with this hunky Wally Underson, Walt Underson's son. Plus, we met his daughter, Gillian. She must be the smartest girl in the world. She has a photographic memory. She had already mastered the Hawaiian language and our history."

The royals gossiped and caught up on the League of Nations and what had gone on about the activities they did in the queen's absence. They were all happy to be together again.

As the motorcade arrived at Iolani Palace, Ryan and Lizzy ran out to greet them.

Maili jumped on Lizzy, and they fell into the grass. Bethany looked at Elizabeth and said, "Old people are so weird."

The two best friends laughed and hugged; they fell to the ground laughing until Ryan helped them up. The rest of the Schildmeyers came out of the palace to greet 'Auntie Maili'.

Ryan asked if they could meet after supper to discuss the latest political events. The main topic is the aggression in the Pacific of the Empire of Japan.

Chapter 27 - The Masquerade Ball

Halloween Night, 1935

Iolani Palace was lit up with orange-flickering torches. It appeared from afar to look like a big square jack-o-lantern. Lizzy and Maili had enjoyed celebrating holidays since they were children. Tonight was no different.

Guests from all over Hawaii were invited to the masquerade ball hosted by Queen Maili. Chiefs and their wives, mayors, businessmen, generals, and admirals from the Hawaiian and US militaries attended.

The US military had doubled security with the number of high-level attendees. Over 100 soldiers were stationed inside the palace walls and just outside the Iolani as well.

Queen Maili's security had all been given the night off so they could attend. As before, they had a special surprise for the queen and her guests.

The sun had set, and the guests began to arrive. The queen and the two princesses were in the queen's bedroom, putting on their final touches.

Bethany was sitting in front of a mirror as Elizabeth finished her green makeup. "Your eyes are greener than this makeup, sister, but you do look pretty creepy."

"Thank you, Dr. Frankenstein. You made me after all." Elizabeth was wearing a white lab coat with fake glasses and gloves. The girls had sewn costumes for Genny and Jelly. They wrapped the wiener dogs in a cloth that looked like a bun with a yellow and red string. Their little legs poked out the sides, and they both looked like hot dogs.

Maili came out of the restroom. Bethany froze with her mouth agape. "Mother! Oh my, you look just like Pele in my dream!"

Maili was wearing a form-fitting, bright orange dress with long black gloves and black shoes. Her face was painted orange with black lines that looked like cracked lava. She elevated her masquerade mask to cover her face. "What do you think, girls?"

Elizabeth said, "Momma, you are the creepiest and most attractive Pele I have ever seen."

There was a knock at the door. "It's us, Lizzy and Ryan."

"One second," Maili requested. "Girls, let's line up so they can see us all at once." The costumed wahines scrambled over to a spot in front of the door and said, "Come in."

As Lizzy opened the door, they all screamed with joy at seeing each other's costumes. Lizzy and

Ryan looked like perfect Raggedy Ann and Andy dolls.

Lizzy pointed at them and laughed. "Look at you three. You are so precious. And, Your Majesty, roowr!" Lizzy made a cat-scratching motion. "The guests are arriving. Let's slip through the back to see if we can mingle without them knowing who we are."

There was another knock at the door. "In Dracula's voice, "Vee vould like to come in."

"Oh, the kids are here! Lizzy opened the door to more screams of joy. Kenny was dressed in a gorilla suit as King Kong, and Emily was in a dress as Ann Darrow with a mask. Charlie had elastic bandages all over her as the Mummy. James was Dracula, and Hannah was a cowgirl.

After another knock on the door, Wally and Gillian appeared dressed as the Lone Ranger and Tonto.

Emily said, "Oh, Wally, you look so handsome. And Gillian, you are Tonto, right?"

In her Tonto voice, "This is Kemosabee! That means a faithful friend. Tonto has multiple meanings. In Potawatomi, it meant scout; in

Espaniol, it meant fool. I'm going with the Potawatomi."

Bethany looked at Maili and said, "See, Mother, I told you she's the smartest girl in the world."

After a few minutes of admiring one another, the group snuck down the back stairs and through the kitchen to mingle with the guests. The fun of masquerade parties is trying to guess who everyone is. Maili got to be a normal person for a while until people started to figure out that Pele was the queen.

A man dressed as Zorro had been staring at Pele for some time. She caught him gawking more than once but did not know who he was. Pele also noticed a bearded man dressed as Al Capone. He was wearing a large-brimmed hat, a pinned-stripe suit, and a Tommy gun. Security had double-checked it before he could enter.

At 8 o'clock, hors d'oeuvres and drinks had been served, and it was time for the show. Pele's true identity was finally revealed as she sat in the Queen's Chair on the patio. Pele sat down and lowered her mask. The guests applauded as Maili revealed her orange and black face. The twins stood at her side.

Zorro whispered to himself, "I knew that was her."

The drums began to beat loudly. Several servants ran to take away the tiki torches, and the gardens became nearly pitch black. The faint city street lamps gave just enough light to show the silhouettes of the palm trees and large bushes.

Loud footsteps could be heard, and a spotlight lit up four actors. The creature on the left appeared to be an octopus. Next to him was a Hawaiian god with a long wooden face and a creepy, long smile. Bethany hugged her mother and said, "Mother, that looks just like Milu in my nightmares. Maili held on to her forearm. Genny and Jelly became frightened and ran back into the palace.

In the middle of the stage was a large Polynesian goddess with the face of the moon. On the far right was a large reptilian god.

The four danced and stomped to the beat of the tropical drums for a few minutes, and then, STOMP! The spotlight went out. Footsteps could be heard. The spotlight came back to center stage.

There stood Kanaloa, the god of the sea. He came in the form of an octopus. "My Queen, my princesses, kanes, and wahines, heed my warning! I am Kanaloa! The ocean is my realm. I will share it with you. I share its bounty with you. However, tread lightly in my realm. Fish when you need to.

Use my waters as a passage for your ships. It will protect you from foreigners, but not for long. One day, when you are sleeping, a threat from far away will come from the skies to destroy you.

The man in the Zorro costume wondered how Kanaloa could possibly know such things.

A general and an admiral watching the show looked at each other with curiosity.

Kanaloa strided over to Zorro and pointed in his face, saying, "You need to be ready for that day, Zorro!"

Zorro began to sweat, feeling the stares of the crowd.

Kanaloa stomped over to Raggedy Andy and pointed in his face, "YOU! Raggedy Andy, how did you like the mahi mahi I prepared for you tonight?" The audience laughed.

"Quite delicious." Ryan quipped.

Kanaloa replied as if he were Groucho Marx: "I thought it was a bit too salty." The audience laughed again. Kanaloa slid back into line and kneeled.

Elizabeth whispered to her mother, "Kanaloa sounded a lot like Izzy." Maili looked at her and winked.

The large reptilian god stomped forward and raised his fists with two large tuna. "I am Ku'ula. I am the god of the fishermen. Pray to me for a great bounty, not that other guy."

The audience erupted with laughter. "I will bring the fish, the tasty crabs, and the seaweed to you." Ku'ula bounded over to Al Capone, "Here hold these, will ya?" Al had to give his Tommy gun to Zorro as he clumsily held on to the slippery tuna. The crowd laughed again.

"My Queen, I will always provide the ono mahi mahi for you and the puka shells that look so lovely around your neck." The crowd applauded, and Ku'ula ran back into line and kneeled.

Large stomping sounds directed the spotlight back to the middle of the stage. In a deep and bellowing female voice, she said, "I am HINA, Goddess of the Moon and the Night," and quietly said, "and fertility. It is said that if I touch you, you shall be the next to have children." Hina started to slither over to Maili, pointing her finger.

Maili curled up in a ball and shouted, "Don't you dare!" Hina teased and got close, but didn't touch the queen. She shuffled over to the princesses, then headed back to the line and kneeled, much to the amusement of the crowd.

The spotlight turned to Milu. "I am the god of chaos; the god of the underworld and demons." His long, ugly face and sinister smile gave Bethany the creeps. She cowered behind her mother. Milu could see the fear in Bethany's actions. Small little children dressed as demons ran across the stage, screeching.

"I am MILU! I come to you in your dreams!" He pointed at Elizabeth. His eyes became red, and all the children present—even some adults—became scared.

"I come as a warning to you," said Princess Elizabeth. "You must tread lightly when you ride!"

Elizabeth leaned over to Bethany and asked, "Did you tell anyone about your dream?" Bethany shrugged innocently.

Milu threw something on the ground, which created small explosions. Then she screeched a loud, crazed cry! The audience began to step back. He slowly shuffled back into line to take a knee.

Kanaloa stepped forward and said, "That concludes our show. I hope you had a laugh and a chill. After all, it is Halloween." He took off his mask. "I am Izzy."

Ku'ula stepped forward and took off his reptile head. "I am Savita. The audience continued to applaud.

Hina walked forward and bowed, to thunderous applause. She took off her moon head and said, "I am Sommy!"

Milu approached the princesses, bowed, and took off his wooden face. "I am Maka!"

Elizabeth said, "I knew it was you."

Zorro was fuming. He gave Al Capone the Tommy Gun. The crowd began to disperse. Zorro walked over to Maili, bowed directly in front of Maka, and said, "Aloha, My Queen. May I kiss your hand?"

"Oh, what a dashing gentleman." Maili held out her hand. Zorro looked at Maka and kissed her hand. Maka could not contain his jealousy and stepped closer. Maili asked, "Who are you, my masked gentleman?"

Just as Zorro was about to reveal himself, Al Capone hustled over and said, "Aloha, Maili."

Maili bounced up, "Austen? Is that you?"

Al Capone took off his mask. "Yes, My Queen."
Maili hugged Austen. "Oh my, Austen, you smell
like fish. When did you arrive?"

Before he could answer, Maili looked to her right.
It was Hideki. He had taken off his Zorro mask.
"Hideki, oh dear!"

Maka breached the circle and said, "Your Majesty,
is there anything I can do for you?"

Maili giggled at the situation: "Maka, you scared
the girls."

Elizabeth barked, "Yes, how did you know about
my dream?"

Maka bowed. "My Princess, I know many things."
He stared at Hideki and Austen with a sneer.

The twins were standing close behind the queen.
Elizabeth leaned into Bethany and said, "This is
getting good."

"Alo, oh my," Raggedy Ann said as she
approached. Lizzy caught on to the awkward
situation and said, "Maka, what an amazing
performance. Hideki, Aloha. Austen, welcome
back."

"Mahalo, Miss Lizzy." Maka replied.

Maili looked at Maka, then at Austen, then at Hideki, and said, "Ummm, I think I am going to get some punch with my friend, Lizzy. Princesses, perhaps you can catch up with your father."

Maili and Lizzy quickly scampered away.

Austen realized he was standing next to his daughters. "Oh, my goodness. You are the two most precious young ladies I have ever seen, even in that hideous makeup, Bethany." He chuckled. "May I hug you both?"

"Of course, Father." The awkward situation continued. Neither Maka nor Hideki were willing to step away. They stayed, listening and chatting with the twins.

Lizzy asked Maili, "How did that happen?"

"I have no idea. First Maka was there, and then Hideki and Austen just showed up. That was the craziest and most awkward moment in my life."

"When did Austen arrive?" Lizzy asked as she drank her punch.

"You got me. It would have been nice to know. That man! He is trying to win my heart, but, Lizzy, there is no spark left. I'd prefer he stay in England. I guess he didn't get the clue when we visited a few months ago."

"Men can be clueless sometimes." Lizzy preached.

Ryan snuck up behind Lizzy and frightened her. "What was that, my dear? Men can be what?"

"Oh, nothing, darling." Lizzy wrapped Ryan's hands around her waist.

Maili smiled and said, "You two are so adorable. I want to be in love again like that someday. I think I need to retire to my bedroom before the night gets even crazier. Lizzy, please help distract the boys while I sneak away."

"Ryan, come with me, please. I may need your help. You and Austen can catch up while I am dealing with Hideki and Maka."

Chapter 28 - A Dangerous Ride

The Koolau Mountains, April 17, 1936

Bethany and Elizabeth drove up to their Royal Horse Ranch in the foothills of the Koolau Mountains. Looking south, the girls could see Pearl Harbor and downtown Honolulu.

Bethany had been riding her horse for five years. She called her Arabian Milu. Riding was her way of dealing with the fear she had in her dreams, and Milu had moments of unpredictability. Milu was a

15-hand pure white Arabian. Bethany's trainer, Debi, had instructed Bethany years ago that Arabians were spirited and needed firmness. It was great practice to rule more powerful creatures than she was. Milu was quite fast and had increased his stamina while running the hills of Koolau.

Macie Lou was a cowgirl who had come to Hawaii after living on a little ranch in Aurora, Colorado, outside of Denver, where she attended to her horses on a daily basis. When Macie Lou was just 13, her aunt Debi asked her to come out for a summer to help on the Royal Ranch. She loved it so much that she decided to come back at 16 and never left. Macie Lou took immaculate care of Milu and Elizabeth's horse, Lio. Lio actually means horse in Hawaiian, so Bethany would tease Elizabeth about her lack of originality.

Elizabeth rode Lio less and less in time. So one day Princess Elizabeth told Macie Lou, "Macie Lou, since you have taken such great care of Lio and Milu, I would like to thank you by giving you Lio as a token of our appreciation."

Macie Lou was speechless. Tears began to roll down her cheeks. Macie Lou had never been given such a gift.

Elizabeth asked, "You are okay with Lio?"

"Oh, Princess, yes, and she wrapped her arms around Lio's neck. Mahalo, Princess."

"There is a catch. You can't tell your Aunt Debi just yet or the security team, and especially not the queen."

"I don't understand, Princess."

Bethany chimed in, "Elizabeth doesn't want Mother to find out she's riding a motorcycle."

Elizabeth used to ride horses but fell in love with a 1934 *Indian Chief* motorcycle. Two older twins ran the maintenance at the horse ranch and tinkered in the barn on their two motorcycles. Jerry and Joe began educating Elizabeth on the nuances of riding a motorcycle. Joe stopped riding after a bad crash, but he loved working on his bike. He would eventually donate it to the princess. Elizabeth became quite knowledgeable about motorcycles and knew the difference between a two-stroke and a four-stroke engine, shifting, braking, and horsepower. She would often work on the bike, but she had to work diligently on getting her hands clean so as not to alert the queen.

Bethany asked, "Why do you keep riding that contraption? You're going to get killed by it one day. Remember my dreams. Pele told me to watch over you."

"Pele knows I ride motorcycles. I'm more famous in the afterlife than I thought." Elizabeth said it with a smirk.

"Let's hope you don't visit for some time, Princess Dum Dum. You are the only sister I have."

"Ow!" Bethany grabbed her lower back.

Elizabeth asked, "What's the matter, Kupunawahine (grandmother)?"

"Oh, I tweaked my back at dance class last night."

"Why don't you stop wasting your time with stupid dances and come join me in karate class?"

"Dear Sister, I am going to be the best hula dancer in all of Hawaii one day. My seductive moves will woo any kane I choose." Bethany bragged.

"Well, Princess Dummy, I will be able to beat up any kane I want. Men respect that."

"I will one day seduce the most handsome kane in Hawaii, and we shall ride off on my stallion into the sunset. You're Kane will be knocked out as you drag him on that contraption." Bethany laughed at Elizabeth.

Elizabeth crossed her arms and thought for a moment, "OK, Princess Dummy, how about we race to Waimano Falls? The last one has to do the other's chores for a week. Unless you're scared to lose to Princess Dum Dum."

"Go fill up your tank. I'll see you at the gate in five minutes!" Bethany accepted the challenge. She knew the Kona Low that had passed through a few days before would make the trails muddy and tough to navigate on a motorcycle.

The twins kept their plans a secret, except for telling Macie Lou. She was a bit older, and they respected and trusted her. She watched from the arena. Telling their plan to any other employees on the ranch would certainly get back to the queen. That would mean being grounded for days.

"To make this fair," Bethany said, "we will both start from the ground." Bethany knew she and Milu could be at full speed in five to ten seconds. Elizabeth always struggled to kick-start her motorcycle, which she called 'Lono', the God of Thunder".

"On your mark, get set, go!" Bethany climbed up on Milu, and they were off galloping away at full speed. Elizabeth took four attempts to kick-start Lono. Within a few more seconds, she was not far behind and gaining ground.

As they climbed the trail, it became narrower and muddier. Bethany slowed down Milu to make sure he could navigate the slippery turns. Elizabeth used this opportunity to gain more ground on her sister.

The race was only a couple of miles, a distance Milu could easily handle. They headed for one of the sharpest turns of the trail. As they approached the falls, Milu suddenly locked his front legs. He slid for several feet, and Bethany tried desperately to hold on but eventually flew over Milu's head, yet she held onto the reins, which prevented her from falling off the edge of the cliff. A tree had fallen onto the path, and not negotiating the turn meant dropping off a hundred-foot cliff.

Bethany heard Lono's engine approaching. She sprung out of the mud and sloshed back down the trail a few feet until Elizabeth could be seen just a few yards around the turn. Bethany waved, but Elizabeth couldn't stop. The only thing Bethany could think of was to protect her twin sister, like Pele foretold. She stood in the way, causing Lono and Elizabeth to partially run Bethany over as she tried to tackle her twin sister.

Bethany was blasted back into the mud, and Lono flew straight off the cliff. It hit hundreds of feet away and tumbled down the mountain. Elizabeth lay teetering on the edge of the cliff, stuck in some vines. Her head was pointing straight down. She was partially dangling 100 feet above the valley.

Within seconds, Elizabeth's last memory before passing out was the sensation of an extremely strong hand grabbing her ankle.

A few minutes later, both of them lay in the mud. Bethany came too, and she started blubbering like a child, thinking Elizabeth was dead. Her shoulder was writhing in pain. Milu clomped over and snorted. He nibbled on Bethany with his big lips, waking her up even more. "YUCK, Milu! Why are you kissing me?"

"And why are you crying, Bethany? What happened?" Elizabeth wondered aloud.

Bethany lifted her face out of the mud and said, "Oh, thank you, Pele; she's alive. Milu saved me from going over the cliff. So I tried to warn you, but you came up too fast. My only thought was to stop you from going over the cliff."

"Thanks, Sister. My neck is killing me!" Elizabeth rubbed her neck.

"My shoulder is killing me! I may have broken my arm." Bethany winced as she spoke.

"Where's Lono?" Elizabeth asked as she sloshed through the mud.

Elizabeth tried to wipe the mud from her face. She had a mouthful and was spitting it out. She continued to rub her neck as she looked over the cliff. She could see across the green valley and Waimano waterfall, a mile away. Lono looked to be a hundred yards down the hill. "I'm screwed!" A defeated Elizabeth moaned.

Bethany limped over and held on to her arm. "Help me get up on Milu, and I'll get us home." Then Bethany noticed, "Hey, who moved the tree off the trail?"

Elizabeth looked at the tree and said, "That tree? No one could move that. It's too heavy, Dummy."

"Princess Dum Dum, I know that. The tree blocked the trail. Look at the drag marks in the mud. That's why Milu bucked me."

"Princess Dummy, I just thought of something. The last thing I remember as I flew off the bike was that

I was looking right over the edge of the cliff, and someone grabbed my ankle and pulled me back."

"Wow! Elizabeth, look at this! FOOTPRINTS! It looks like someone was here and pushed the tree off to the side of the road."

Bethany said, "This is too weird. Who has the strength to do that? Look how wide and deep those footprints are. Those aren't normal footprints, Elizabeth! Let's get out of here."

"You can control Milu with one arm?" Elizabeth asked.

"I could ride Milu naked, blindfolded, with two broken arms, and get us home."

"I'd like to see that." Elizabeth smiled as she hopped up on the back of Milu.

"What are we going to tell Mother?" Bethany asked.

"Remember when Momma told us about the time she and Lizzy got into trouble on Maui? She told the truth and was spared worse punishment. I think we should go that route."

"OW! My shoulder and my back are killing me. I agree. Let's tell the truth and take our punishment like strong wahines."

As the girls made their way back down the trail, Debi and Macie Lou could see them both on Milu a couple hundred yards away. They knew there had been trouble. Macie Lou and Debi jumped on their saddles and rode their horses at full speed to get to the girls. "Oh my, you two are covered in mud. What happened?" Debi asked.

"We both had a little accident."

"Let me ride back and call for an ambulance." Debi said, "Macie Lou, stay with them and get them to the arena!"

"You'd better call Mother." Bethany said. That was a phone call Debi dreaded.

An hour later...

The girls both arrived at a military hospital in Pearl Harbor about an hour before Maili, Emily, and Lizzy.

Old Doctor Barnes was checking his clipboard and shuffled up to the queen, saying, "The girls were admitted and both taken to get X-rays. Bethany has a broken clavicle, and Elizabeth has bruised ribs

212

and a sprained neck. They will both be fine, and I expect a full recovery. Nurse Korbett will escort them into their rooms. They are pretty shaken, so go easy on them, please."

Maili wasn't used to having people tell her what to do, but in this case, it was 'the doctor's orders.'

Emily was the first to enter the room as Maili signed some paperwork. She looked at Izzy, at Macie Lou, and then at the twins. "Oh Bethany, Elizabeth, are you two alright?"

They both shook their heads and said, 'yes'. They were still caked in dried mud.

Bethany asked, "Is Mother upset?"

Emily whispered, "She hasn't said a word."

Elizabeth looked up and said, "Oh no!"

Izzy opened the door for the queen and Lizzy. Emily and Macie Lou were sitting by their sides. "Izzy, can you tell me what happened?"

Izzy bowed in shame and said, "My Queen, I was not present."

"What security detail was there?" Maili demanded.

"I was on duty, but the girls asked me to go ride into the mountains, and I am not skilled in horseback riding or motorcycles." Izzy continued to look down. He had never disappointed the queen before.

"Motorcycle? MOTORCYCLE? Who was riding a motorcycle?" Maili stared at Elizabeth. Maili rarely raised her voice, and it had been years since she had become angry with the twins.

"Momma!" Elizabeth whimpered.

"ADDRESS ME AS YOUR QUEEN IN PUBLIC, PRINCESS! What happened?"

Elizabeth stuck to her word and told the entire story.

Maili crossed her arms and sighed, "So let me get this straight. Elizabeth, you went against my command and continued to ride that motorcycle. And you, Bethany, knew and kept something so dangerous from me? And you, Miss Macie Lou, knew as well?"

Macie Lou's eyes filled with tears as tear after tear fell down her cheeks. Macie Lou had never been more ashamed.

The twins' bright eyes had become red and filled with tears.

"IZZY! You knew of this atrocity?"

Izzy continued to kneel, saying, "I was unaware, Your Majesty. We thought she was riding a horse like her sister."

Maili continued to stare. "So you lied to your security details too?"

Bethany was sniffling. "My Queen, do you remember when you and Miss Lizzy snuck out on Maui as children? You told the truth, and Queen Lydia showed mercy. Won't you do the same for us?"

"Sneaking out to the ocean at 10 years old and lying about riding a motorcycle at 15 are two different things." Maili shot back.

"No disrespect, My Queen, but didn't the two of you almost die too?"

Lizzy leaned in and whispered, "She's got you there."

Maili attempted not to smile as she looked into Lizzy's eyes. Maili regained focus. "IZZY, prepare the dungeon!" Maili and Lizzy stormed out of the room.

"Yes, My Queen." Izzy looked back at the princesses and said, "Oh, princesses, you are in BIG trouble." The twins looked at each other in horror.

Maili whispered to Lizzy, "Now that's what I call acting."

Lizzy replied, "The dungeon was a great idea. They'll be crying for hours."

Emily looked at the twins and asked, "The palace has a dungeon."

"MOTHER!" Bethany shouted. "Please come back."

Maili turned around and went through the door, but she said nothing as she got back into character.

"There's more to the story." Bethany looked at Elizabeth through her tears and said, "Something kind of weird happened up on the mountain." Her lower lip was still quivering. "You see, the reason we crashed was because of a fallen tree on the muddy trail. Elizabeth almost fell off the cliff, but someone pulled her back. Then someone moved the tree, which was way too heavy for a human to move. We saw really weird footprints where the tree was, but no people."

Maili's and Lizzy's eyes opened wide as they slowly turned towards each other. "We will talk about this later."

Lizzy leaned in close to Maili and said, "Menehunes, right? What else, or who else could do such things?"

Maili remembered Aunt Lydia told her long ago that the Menehune would often repair roads after storms. The natives never knew why.

"My security team is going to get a tongue-lashing tonight!"

Later that evening at the palace...

Maili's security team was called for an emergency meeting. The members were sitting around the queen's table, and no one was talking—a rare event.

Maili marched in and sat abruptly. Lizzy and Ryan followed closely behind her.

Maili cleared her throat. "Izzy, you are captain of my security, are you not?"

Izzy quietly said, "Yes, My Queen."

"Who do you serve?"

"You, my queen."

"Maka, Sommy, Savita, Tatu, who do you serve?"

"In unison, they all replied, "You, My Queen."

"Well, that's peculiar, because the heirs to the throne are in the hospital and almost died today, and NO ONE IN MY SECURITY DETAIL KNEW OF THEIR WHEREABOUTS, OR THAT ELIZABETH WAS RIDING A MOTORCYCLE?" Maili looked around the table as every member had a look of shame. "So either you knew and kept it from me, which is a fireable offense, or the heirs to the throne are running around Oahu like wild wahines without supervision, which is also a fireable offense!" There was silence. "Let me get something perfectly clear! If you withhold information like this from me again, you will be fired, and if my daughters, the heirs to the throne, get hurt, I will sentence you to be tortured in our dungeon! Do I make myself clear?"

"Yes, My Queen," they said in unison.

Maili stormed out of the room with Lizzy and Ryan.

Tatu leaned over to Izzy and said, "We have a dungeon?"

Chapter 29 - War on the Horizon

US Army Headquarters, Pearl Harbor, January 16, 1938

Japanese aggression concerned almost every nation in the Pacific. The military leaders of the United States, Hawaii, the Philippines, Australia, China, and Indonesia all flew into Hawaii to discuss a plan of action.

Japan invaded Manchuria, northern China, in 1931. The League of Nations condemned this action; however, Japan failed to yield to the League's requests.

By July 1937, Japan had launched a full invasion of China. Some of the worst atrocities ever known were committed against civilians in December 1937. The city of Nanjing was bombed. Japan's goal was to subjugate the Chinese people and gain more territory for their fascist leaders.

Once again, the world and the League of Nations cried out for the torture and murder to stop, but the Japanese continued their assault on the Chinese people.

The meeting at Pearl Harbor was with US Army General Andrew Moses and his assistant, Walt Underson. The US Navy admiral in charge of the Pacific Fleet was Husband Kimmel. Accompanying him was US Ambassador to Hawaii Logan Mitchell. The new Philippine President, Manuel Quezon, attended along with Chinese Premier Chaing Kai-Shek. Also attending from the Southern Pacific were Prime Minister Joseph Lyons from Australia. The last to arrive at the meeting were Queen Maili Kaanapali and her twin daughters, Princess Bethany and Princess Elizabeth.

General Moses bowed and said, "Welcome, Your Highnesses. Our purpose today is to unite our militaries and to prepare for growing aggression from the fascist Japanese." Moses pointed to Kimmel.

"Aloha everyone, The United States has increased its spending on the Navy; however, the lasting economic depression has slowed the growth of the number of ships needed to defend against a growing Japanese threat. President Roosevelt is a naval man, but we are strapped by Congressional budgets."

Chiang Kai-Shek raised his hand and spoke in a strong Cantonese accent: "I must encourage all of you to prepare for the incoming storm. The Japanese will not stop. Their goal is to have an empire larger than the British. I would predict the Philippines, Indonesia, and even Hawaii are all at risk. I can tell you they have no morals. They torture, murder, and rape our civilians daily."

President Quezon of the Philippines responded in impeccable English, "Admiral Kimmel, we do not have a navy to defend our many islands. Can we get assistance from the US Navy? The Filipino people would hope for a small fleet of destroyers and a cruiser."

Kimmel shuffled his papers and said, "We are stretched very thin, Mr. President, but we will increase patrols in that area to let the Japanese know we are present."

Prime Minister Lyons of Australia spoke in a strong Australian accent and said, "Great Britain has promised more naval assistance. However, they are getting requests from India and South Africa. We will be lucky to get more than a few ships. That will not be enough if Japan brings its main naval force."

"Your Majesties, do you feel secure here in Hawaii?" Moses asked.

Queen Maili had prepared the twins, and Bethany spoke first: "When Japan last attacked, they only sent one ship. We are sure they will not make that mistake again. Our ancestors say they will attack from the air." The men looked at each other, puzzled. "We hope we can increase aircraft for defense."

General Moses replied, "We have over 100 aircraft ready for that event. We have sold the Hawaiian Air Force 20 planes as well." Bethany nodded in approval.

Elizabeth offered an idea: "Why don't we approach Tojo and Yamamoto as a unified body? We could say we are aware of the aggression, and we will all act to defend ourselves and each other if attacked." Maili nodded.

General Moses looked around the room at the nods of agreement. Impressed with the twins' political savvy, he said, "Wonderful ideas, Your Majesties. I would say we should move on this right away."

The news of the royals' leadership skills made international news.

One week later...

At Tokyo Military Headquarters, General Hideki Tojo approached the Admiral and said, "Admiral Yamamoto, several nations in the Pacific appear to be rallying to create a defense against us. We must act quickly." Hideki Tojo warned.

"HAI! I, too, am concerned about this news. We are many months away from our plan. If we are not at full strength, it is likely to fail. I will need every airplane available for this to succeed. We will need to divert them from China without raising suspicions, unless we can produce four to five hundred more in the next year." Yamamoto replied.

Emperor Hirohito quietly stated, "Gentlemen, we attempted this before, and it was a major failure. Now that the Americans are involved, I fear they will rise against us. This could be devastating to Nippon and my citizens."

Standing at attention, Tojo insisted, "With all due respect, Your Highness, this plan will strike with such a blow that there will be no one to oppose us for years."

Hirohito exhaled, "The United States is not China. Is Hitler's plan still on schedule?"

"My Emperor, it appears Hitler and Mussolini will have fooled Chamberlain of England and Deladier of France within just a few months. Their plan for expanding east is on schedule. That will occupy the Americans enough for us to accomplish our ultimate plan of conquering all of the Pacific."

Chapter 30 - Hideki and Maka

Hideki's Residence, Honolulu, Oahu, September 3, 1939

Hideki folded the newspaper in half. He knew the world would never be the same. The world was at war. Hideki's home country was at war with China, and the war was expanding. Italy had invaded Ethiopia, and now Nazi Germany had invaded Poland. France and Great Britain had just declared war on Germany. Soon, millions of people would die.

Hideki had arranged a lunch meeting with Lizzy Doel, his old childhood friend. He needed advice on re-establishing a relationship with the queen. It would not be easy. Maili was an intelligent, strong, and stubborn woman.

There was a knock on his door. "Telegram."

Hideki looked through the peephole; it appeared legitimate.

"Yes?"

A telegram for Hideki Yamamoto."

"That's me." Hideki took the letter and said, "Arigato." The man looked at him strangely.

Hideki opened up the letter. It said just two words:

'Tiger Shark'.

Hideki closed the door and placed his back on it. It was as if the weight of the Pacific Ocean was slowly driving him down until he was in a fetal position. Hideki found himself torn between duty to the Emperor of Japan and his love for the Queen of Hawaii.

A few hours later...

Lizzy agreed to meet Hideki at a local coffee house. She felt it was inappropriate and unsafe to meet a man alone, but it would be in public, and she thought Hideki was worth the risk.

Hideki was sitting at a table on the sidewalk, drinking tea, when Lizzy approached. "Good afternoon, Hideki. It is so nice to see you."

"Lizzy, thank you for coming. Can I get you some coffee or tea?"

"That would be lovely, Hideki. Tea please. So what's this all about?"

"I know we haven't been close in forever, but I would like to ask a favor. I want to reconnect with Maili—I mean, Queen Maili. I thought that if you broached the subject with her, you could save me the embarrassment of having to be rejected publicly."

Lizzy thought for a moment: "You know, Hideki, I am not sure either one of us has forgiven you for what you did to poor little Coconut, and after all of this time, why meet her now?"

"Oh my, Lizzy. I am so sorry. I was a young, stupid, drunk kid. I still think of that party. What a nightmare. Now, here we are... Coconut's gone,

Queen Lydia's gone, Koa's gone, and Po is gone. It makes me so sad. As for Maili, Hideki looked deep into Lizzy's eyes as his filled with tears. "I have never gotten over her, Lizzy."

"I can see that, Hideki." She thought for a moment and decided to give Hideki some grace. "I still can't believe what happened to Po. Communism changed him for the worse." Lizzy was saddened by her memories.

"Can I be honest with you, Lizzy?"

"Of course, Hideki."

"Po was certifiable. I mean, crazy. I know he loved you and Maili. But all he talked about was killing off the monarchy. He mentioned once what Lydia did to his family—you know, with Kalaupapa and the Chinatown Fire. He blamed Lydia and wanted to take it out on Maili. Have you heard of this guy, Mao Zedong, in China?"

"Oh, yes."

"He took advantage of Po's hatred of the monarchy. The communists are whacko too. Everyone who has succeeded in life is garbage to them. Anyway, I could ramble on about politics forever. Do you think you can put in a good word to Maili for me?"

"Of course I can, but Hideki, you just appeared out of nowhere, and then we didn't see you for months. I don't think the queen trusts you. She's a great judge of character and the things the twins dream about! Their dreams come true all the time. Recently, Bethany has dreamt of bombs falling from the sky."

Hideki looked stone-faced and thought, "How does she foresee the future?"

The two childhood friends talked for an hour until Ryan showed up. "Hello Dear. Aloha Hideki. Are you ready, sweetheart? The kids are waiting for you at supper."

"I will let you know what she says." Lizzy stated. Hideki stood and bowed. Then Hideki ordered more tea and some cookies. Hideki imagined himself on Pali Point. Strong winds were pushing near the edge of the cliff. Should he run with the pressure of duty to the emperor and jump, or should he fight the cyclone-force winds for his queen? His mind was racing, and he began thinking to himself, "I will let fate decide Maili's future. If she chooses me, I will inform her of Japan's plans. If she rejects me, Operation *Tiger Shark* will proceed."

Later that evening, after dinner...

Lizzy asked if she could talk to the queen privately out in the garden.

Lizzy and Maili strolled along the flowery pathway as they had done so many times in the past. Today, a few feet behind them was Maka.

Lizzy asked, "Guess who I had lunch with today?"

Maili thought for a second, "Hmmm, Shirley Temple?"

"No, silly, Hideki." Maka's attention peaked. Maili looked back and made brief eye contact with Maka.

"What brought this on? I haven't seen him in months."

"Well, apparently he wants to rekindle a relationship with you, but he didn't want to get rejected in public. So he asked me, as an old friend, to ask if you would be interested."

"I wonder why after all these years?" Maili asked.

"My queen, have you looked in the mirror lately? You are the most ravishing wahine in Hawaii. He'd be crazy not to be interested. Plus, he did save your life. I guess you at least owe him lunch." Lizzy gently elbowed her friend. Lizzy was unconcerned that Maka was listening.

Maili peaked again. Maka was looking down. "I tell you what, Miss Lizzy Schildmeyer, Chamberlain of the Palace, tell him the three of us can have lunch out here in the garden next week."

Hannah approached the two old friends, followed closely by Jelly, and said, "Mother, my queen, dessert is ready. Please come and join us."

Maili patted her stomach. I am stuffed. You go ahead. I'll be in right after a little stroll."

Lizzy held Hannah's hand, and they skipped back towards the palace, followed closely now by Genny and Jelly. Lizzy looked back and saw peculiar body language between Maili and Maka. She began to remember other occasions when they were a little closer together than the other guards, and it suddenly dawned on her. She smiled a happy smile and continued skipping.

Chapter 31 - Fight for Her Majesty's Hand

The Queen's Dining Room, February 14, 1940

It was Valentine's Day, and the royals were eating breakfast. Romance was in the air. Queen Maili was playing with her food. Something was weighing heavily on her mind.

"What's the matter, Momma?" Elizabeth asked.

She twirled her fork in her ramen and said, "Oh, nothing."

Elizabeth looked at Bethany. Bethany and Elizabeth were talking about their dates for the evening. They sensed this had something to do with the queen's sadness. Elizabeth dropped a scrap of ham on the patient, Jelly.

"Mother, will you be my Valentine?" Bethany asked.

Maili looked up and attempted a smile. "Of course, My Precious." Maili looked back down at her plate. Bethany and Elizabeth looked at each other with great sadness.

"Excuse us, Mother, we need to leave." Bethany motioned Elizabeth into the next room. "We need to do something. I've never seen Mother so distraught."

Elizabeth asked, "Maybe Auntie Lizzy can help us?" The girls made their way to Lizzy's office. "Auntie Lizzy, may we talk to you privately?"

"Of course, Your Majesties, what can I do for you?" Lizzy closed her door behind them.

The twins looked at each other, and Bethany began, "The queen is depressed. We have never seen her like this before. What should we do?"

"Hmm, it's Valentine's Day, and I bet she's lonely. I know just the guy to cheer her up. Let me take care of this." Lizzy winked.

In the afternoon, the twins presented the queen with a beautiful bouquet. "Aw, girls, you shouldn't have. That is so sweet."

Izzy appeared before the girls and said, "Your Majesty, there's someone here to see you. May I bring him in?" Maili nodded curiously.

The royal family was chatting idly until Izzy reappeared. Directly behind him was Hideki.

"Hideki! Aloha, what are you doing here?" Maili asked.

Hideki bowed. "I was summoned by you, Your Majesty." Hideki appeared a bit confused.

Maili's face lit up, and Bethany and Elizabeth leaned into one another. Bethany suddenly stepped forward and said, "Perhaps the two of you should begin your stroll around the grounds?"

Hideki asked, "May I escort you, My Queen?" The couple began their stroll around the gardens. They were chatting about the old days.

Lizzy joined the twins. "What seems to be going on here?" she said with a sly grin.

Elizabeth looked into Auntie Lizzy's eyes and said, "It was you, wasn't it?"

"Whatever do you mean, Princess?" Lizzy turned away to hide her smile.

"You sent Hideki here, didn't you?" Elizabeth asked.

Lizzy played dumb, saying, "I am not sure what you are referring to." Lizzy stared into Elizabeth's eyes, expressionless.

"Hmmm, I do believe you do." Elizabeth stared back, trying to get her aunt Lizzy to crack. Elizabeth turned around in a snap and stomped off. She began looking for Maka.

Maili knew she had been set up, but having Hideki there was a great way to uplift her spirits. The two old friends meandered around the gardens until it was nearly time for supper. "Hideki, would you like to stay for supper?"

"That would be tremendous. Thank you for the offer." Hideki began to feel like there was a chance with his old friend. If that were the case, when and how would he broach the subject of *Operation Tiger Shark*?

As Izzy opened the entrance door from the gardens, Maka flew through the air and tackled Hideki. Maka punched Hideki in the face, and they began to wrestle. The attack shocked Hideki, but his training kicked in, and he manipulated Maka's limbs so neither one could strike each other.

Izzy screamed at Maka, "What is the matter with you?" He grabbed the back of his neck, performed a Half-Nelson, and peeled him away from Hideki.

Maili stood in the doorway, shocked and silent.

Izzy pushed Maka away from Hideki and said, "I knew your feelings for the queen were going to create a problem. You are suspended from security details indefinitely; now get off the palace grounds."

Maka continued to grasp for breath from his altercation. He looked back at Maili one last time. His heart was breaking, and his impulsive feelings got the best of him. Maili looked into his eyes with sadness, knowing she would most likely never see her special friend again.

Izzy dusted Hideki off. His mouth was bleeding, and it appeared he was going to have a shiner. "Let's get you inside and clean up those wounds, Mr. Yamamoto."

Hideki saw something in Maili's eyes for the first time as she watched Maka leave. Maili had feelings for Maka. He decided at that point that he wasn't going to pursue her hand until they could have a truthful and intimate conversation.

Above the fray, looking out their upstairs window, were Bethany and Elizabeth. They watched the entire altercation.

"I feel horrible about this. This is entirely your fault." Bethany said.

Elizabeth continued to lean on the window seal with her forearms clutching Jelly. The princess peered out into the gardens. She could see bright pink flowers, deep green plants, large banyan trees, and beyond the city of Honolulu. "It needed to be done. Our queen is the most beautiful whale in Hawaii. She is lonely and needs a man. Her relationship with Maka was inappropriate and needed to be stopped. Besides, Hideki is a much better choice." Elizabeth spoke calmly.

"Elizabeth, you are cold-blooded. Shouldn't Mother choose who she wants to spend her time with, not us?"

"I am cold-blooded only when I need to be. Perhaps you will realize one day that if we are to be queens of these islands, we must do things we never thought we could do. I never thought it would be our responsibility to make Momma happy."

Chapter 32 - FDR and the Royals

Pearl Harbor, Oahu, Hawaii, June 1, 1941

Princess Elizabeth was dreaming again. She was hovering above a man with paralyzed legs. He was making a speech about going to war. This would be the catalyst for the deaths of millions of people.

In an instant, she was hovering over a camp in a forest. Thousands of very emaciated people in striped clothes were working strenuously. A locomotive stopped, and train car after train opened its doors, allowing another thousand people to enter the camp. Children were taken away in trucks as parents fought as hard as they could to hang onto them. She saw smoke coming out of a tall chimney. The smell was hideous, like nothing she'd ever smelled before. She became nauseous.

She woke suddenly. Her bright blue eyes opened wide, and she began to breathe heavily. She was by herself. She looked to her right, but Bethany's bed was gone. She forgot they had finally gotten their own rooms. Elizabeth felt a sense of sadness.

Princess Bethany was dreaming in her room. She could hear familiar voices, even though she could not recognize them. They were familiar voices that she had never heard before. "Princess, millions of people will burn. Fire will consume entire cities. Thousands of men will die on the beaches. Two cities will feel the sun."

Bethany woke up struggling to breathe. Her skin felt as if it were on fire. Her bright emerald eyes opened. She looked to her left, but Elizabeth was not there. She struggled to breathe until she could gather her thoughts, and she told herself it was just another nightmare.

Two hours later...

President Franklin D. Roosevelt's ship had anchored in Pearl Harbor. Thousands of military personnel and Hawaiians came out to greet one of the most powerful men in the world. FDR had been re-elected for a historic third time as President of the United States. His 'New Deal' had challenges, but recently gearing up for war helped bring young men back to the workforce, and the economy had improved tremendously.

Queen Maili, Princess Bethany, Princess Elizabeth, Ryan Schildmeyer, and Walt Underson were waiting for the president to be wheeled down the gangplank. Assistants took great measures to protect the president from the press. They wanted to keep his crippled legs out of the eyes of the public. He had braces to help him stand. After strenuous attempts to stand, the considerate press began taking photographs.

Queen Maili and President Roosevelt reminisced about the last time he was in Hawaii. He was pleasantly surprised at the expansion and improvements at Pearl Harbor. The two leaders posed for a few more photographs and then entered the presidential limousine.

Elizabeth looked at Bethany and said, "That was the man in my dream. He is going to send thousands of men to their deaths."

"I don't think America is going to start a war," Bethany whispered.

"I think he is going to end it," Elizabeth said solemnly.

Franklin and Maili drove around Pearl Harbor to give the president a better perspective of the naval institution.

"This is quite the facility, don't you think, Your Majesty?"

"Mr. President, with your engineers and our workforce, Pearl Harbor can dock multiple battleships, submarines, and so much more. We have moved the aircraft onto other air bases and have underground oil storage in secret locations around the islands." Maili boasted.

"If I may be frank with you, Your Majesty, we have broken some secret codes of the Japanese military. It appears that a major attack is imminent."

"My goodness. Where?" Maili asked.

"We believe in the Philippines, perhaps Indonesia, and possibly here at Pearl Harbor." FDR said as he looked at Maili.

"WHAT? How long have you known this?" Maili became irritated.

"We don't know anything for sure. However, we have lost contact with much of the Japanese fleet. They have gone radio silent. We have many spy planes looking for them, but the Pacific Ocean is so vast. It is surprisingly easy to hide in the wide open ocean." Franklin said as he bit his plastic cigarette filter.

"If there is a possibility of an attack, why are all of these battleships here? Why don't you take them out to sea?" Bethany asked. "My dream said we would be attacked from the air!"

"What the Japanese do not know is that we have two aircraft carriers and their support ships not far from here. We have increased our air support by adding another 100 fighters, and we have a secret weapon on Opana Point!" Roosevelt bragged and tried to calm the royals.

"A secret weapon?" Maili questioned.

"It's called RADAR, a brilliant invention of the British. It sends an electronic beam into the sky. If an airplane is flying within a hundred miles of your island, the beam is reflected back, and we will be able to detect their approach. We will be able to prepare our ships and aircraft to produce quite a formidable defense." FDR beamed with confidence.

Maili became even more irritated: "The Hawaiian military was not informed of this!"

"My apologies; it is of the utmost importance that we keep that a secret. There are Japanese spies here, and we don't want the Japanese to know we will be prepared."

"You want the Japanese to attack?" Elizabeth asked.

"Well, of course not, Your Majesty. But if they do, we will be ready. It will give me the political power to declare war on Japan to help Chiang Kai-shek and China. Then I suppose Hitler will declare war on us because of the Triple Axis agreement, and we can help Churchill in England too. This will thrill your husband, making his company quite lucrative." FDR smiled at Maili.

"His wealth is of zero concern, Mr. President. I think we need to exhaust any other options of diplomacy before we accept that war is inevitable," Maili said.

"With all due respect, it is too late for that. I have cut off all petroleum shipments to them. As much as we need the oil revenue, we cannot justify supporting those murderers."

"I will put our forces on alert." Maili said it sternly.

"I suggest that... Please do not do that, Your Majesty. We want them to come. They will start the war, and we will finish it. If you alert your troops, their espionage agents here will alert Japan."

"What if the radar doesn't alert us? What if they send their entire fleet? Don't they have five or six aircraft carriers? And you just said you don't know where they are?"

I trust our generals and admirals to defend your islands, Queen Maili. Have faith. We have moved all of our aircraft into defendable locations so terrorists cannot destroy them."

FDR and the royals were preparing for World War II. Queen Maili was furious that FDR was using Hawaii as bait, but she knew she didn't have any choice.

Chapter 33 - Hideki's Final Attempt

The Queen's Garden, October 20, 1941

Hideki had been invited to dine with the queen on multiple occasions. Hideki was hoping he could advance his courtship. Either Maili was playing hard to get or she just wasn't interested in the same thing as Hideki. However, they both seemed to enjoy each other's company.

Operation Tiger Shark was approaching. It was so secret that even Hideki didn't know about the final planning stages. Hideki knew he was running out of time to warn the Japanese, or Maili. He figured today's attempt would be his final try at winning her hand. Hideki thought about how little of a player on the world stage he would soon become in the next few days, but also about how big of a decision Maili and ultimately he were about to make.

Hideki decided to take in the moment. The sun beat down on the back of his neck. The warm tropical wind blew through his linen shirt, which was white and adorned with green palm leaves. He stood across the street from Iolani. He stared at the main gate and the coral walls, where years earlier *the Minutemen* had been slaughtered by the Palace Guards. He could look out over the balcony where Po and he watched Maili's coronation. He looked over the walls at the coconut trees and beautiful tropical flowers.

Hideki wondered, "Would the palace look like this in a few months, or would it be flattened by Japanese bombs? Would the Japanese take it over and make it their headquarters? Would there be a Japanese flag flying over it shortly?"

Hideki took a slow, deep breath through his nose. He exhaled and crossed the street. The front guard asked for his identification and checked with his registrar to see if Hideki was on the schedule. "You're good; c'mon in."

After a few minutes, Maili met Hideki out in the Queen's Garden.

"It's rather hot today; would you like some iced tea?" Maili asked politely.

"Oh please." He gulped down half of the glass.

"Thirsty?" Maili teased.

"I am. I stood outside the palace grounds for a while after my walk over."

Maili looked confused. "Why did you do that?"

"I have a feeling I won't be around much longer." Hideki looked out onto the horizon.

Maili touched his shoulder and said, "Hideki, please tell me what's going on."

"Maili, I have known you since I was ten. I had a crush on you then, and it is much more than that now. I thought I made that clear, and you keep rejecting my advances. Do you not care for me?" Hideki looked deep into the queen's brown eyes.

"Sit with me, Hideki." They both pulled up chairs. "Hideki, I care for you very much. I have always known you had feelings for me. But have you forgotten that I am still married to Austen? It is a horrible marriage, but it would not be appropriate to be seen out in public with you, especially with you being Japanese."

"What? Are you racist?" Hideki raised his voice.

"Hideki, please remember who you are talking to." Maili used a different tone as Hideki turned his body towards the palace in disgust. "With the political climate, it would not look good for me to be seen with a Japanese man, and until I have divorced Austen, our relationship must remain as friends."

"Be honest with me, please, My Queen. Do you have feelings for me or not? If you don't, I will not waste any more of your time or mine."

Maili scooted her chair in and moved her face close to Hideki's. Hideki became confused, excited, and uncomfortable.

"Hideki, since I was nine, you have been my hero. I cared for you as a big brother. When we were teenagers, you were my first crush. When you returned from Japan, I was quite confused about how I felt about you. Now, if life were different, I would definitely want to see what a relationship with you would be like."

"Do you mean that?" Hideki cracked a small smile.

"Yes, of course I do. However, Hideki, I am the Queen of Hawaii. I am responsible for more than you can imagine. Because of how I feel about you, I am going to tell you this: So do with this information what you want." Maili paused... took a deep breath and continued, "My secret service has been spying on you for months. I know what you are up to. I didn't want to believe it at first, but I have heard recordings of some incriminating conversations with you and other spies on this island."

Hideki turned pale and became nauseous.

I want you to know that there is a sniper with his sights on you at this very moment. Many in my cabinet don't want me near you, but I love you, Hideki. I want you to be safe, and you are not safe here in Hawaii. I suggest you go back to Japan as quickly as possible. Your life is in danger. I cannot control those who desire to remove you any longer."

Hideki looked back into the most beautiful eyes he'd ever seen. They pierced his heart to the point of actual pain. He almost cried but forced himself to contain his emotions.

"I... appreciate your honesty more than I can say, Your Majesty. I will take your advice to heart." Hideki stood at attention. He turned as he was trained. "HAI!" Like a robot, he spun away and marched like a professional soldier towards the gate of the palace grounds. After a few steps, he abruptly stopped. He thought, "Should I warn her?" Maili looked at him as he stood still. He thought for another moment, staring forward, and Hideki slapped his hips with both hands and marched away.

Izzy, Sommy, Bethany, and Elizabeth approached the queen to console her. "Mother, I am so sorry about your friend." Bethany bent down and wrapped her arms around the queen.

Izzy pardoned himself. "My Queen, what would you have our security detail do now?"

"Watch him. Make sure he makes it on the first ship back to Asia."

Lizzy made her way over to the group and said, "I just heard. Oh, Maili. Let's walk through the gardens." The girls consoled Maili. They knew it would be the last time they would ever see Hideki.

Hideki headed back towards his apartment, only a few blocks south. He kept looking over his shoulder, knowing he was being watched. As he tried to unlock his door, he looked back. The streets of Honolulu were buzzing with shoppers, vendors, and tourists. However, that didn't matter to Hideki.

He entered a small closet in the back bedroom. Inside were his military uniforms and weapons. He had stacks of paperwork that contained sensitive information. He quickly placed them in a metal barrel outside and set them ablaze on his back patio. Hideki went back inside, stripped down to his underwear, and put on his uniform. Everything was perfect, down to the last button.

Hideki kneeled and pulled his wakisashi from its sheath.

He remembered diving into the surf to rescue Princess Maili. It seemed so long ago. He remembered chasing after Maili in the palace gardens as a child. He remembered that fateful going-away party when he forced Coconut off the balcony. He remembered the look on Maili's face when he took off his Zorro mask. His last thought was of being inches away from Maili's face, her eyes, and the smell of plumerias in her hair as she told him the news. Hideki placed the wakisashi above his belly button and closed his eyes. "HAI!"

Chapter 34 - A Date That Will Live in Infamy

The Queen's Dining Room, December 7, 1941

It was 6 a.m. The sun had not risen, but it didn't matter to the twins and the Schildmeyers. Today was the annual picking of the Christmas pineapples.

The morning started with an early breakfast. Maili insisted that if she could not attend, at least she could have breakfast with everyone.

All of the Schildmeyers were in attendance. Maili, Lizzy, and Ryan would begin the Christmas celebration planning after the children left.

A telegram arrived marked 'URGENT'. Maili began to open it.

Bethany asked, "What does it say?"

My Queen,

The Japanese Naval Fleet has been missing for months. An attack on Oahu is imminent. Keep your troops at the ready.

Austen

Elizabeth raised her voice. "That's it? No, how are my daughters? No, I love you!"

"Now, now, Princess. This is not the time for that. Izzy, make sure you and Tatu are fully ready to defend the motorcade should something happen."

Lizzy asked with worry, "Should we keep them home?" The children shouted, "No! No! It's tradition."

Kenny Junior stepped forward and said, "I will watch out for them and protect them should the Japanese try anything. We know where to hide in the jungle."

The kids and their bodyguards drove off, leaving their parents concerned but happy that the next generation was continuing their tradition.

Ryan asked, "What do you make of this? Should we alert the commanders?"

"Yes Ryan. Let's plan an emergency meeting today at noon. Let's do as Austen suggests and prepare the troops. I think we have waited long enough."

5 a.m., Kailua airstrip...

Sommy was kissing Afa Aloha. "Please tell Cousins Ben and Ella Aloha for me. When do you think you'll be home?"

Afa picked up his small suitcase and handed it to the pilot of the small crop duster. He said, Honey, that island is so boring. There is nothing to do there but eat and drink."

"So you may never come back?" Sommy laughed at her own joke.

"Ha! Very funny. Probably two days. Aloha, Honey."

Afa climbed aboard and struggled to fit his large frame into the small compartment behind the pilot. Sommy chuckled as Afa placed a scarf and head gear with glasses on. Pilot Nels Clements flew mail and medical supplies to Niihau a few days a week as a side job. The plane taxied and took off quickly to the northwest on its two-hour flight.

Two hours later...

The phone rang, and Maili's assistant answered and said it sounded important.

Maili said, "Aloha."

"Queen Maili! This is an emergency! You must get to safety!"

Maili recognized the panic in Kenny's voice: "Are the girls ok?"

A loud buzz of airplanes flew over the palace, and the largest boom she'd ever heard came as a bomb landed just yards from the palace. Savita ran to escort Maili to the bomb shelter. Waiting for Maili was Sommy. "Please get in quickly, Your Highness!" She closed the hatch as Savita ran to the weapons locker to get his machine gun.

Wave after wave of Japanese Zeroes flew over, dropping bombs on the ships anchored on Battleship Row. Then the earth shook as if an earthquake had rocked the entire island, knocking Savita off his feet.

The *USS Arizona* had just blown up, killing 1,100 men instantly. Savita was in shock, but with adrenaline at its height, he shot 20 rounds into a Zero that flew directly over the palace. The Zero began to smoke, and it headed back toward the Japanese fleet.

Savita ran to the bomb shelter and knocked on the secret door. Sommy opened it aiming her pistol at the hatch. "Sommy, I am so sorry. *Arizona* just blew up."

Sommy collapsed and began to wail. Sommy's oldest son, Tutu, worked on *The Arizona*.

Near Haeiwa...

Private Marc Peetersun was standing on Kenny's wing, giving him a pep talk as he was revving his engine. He shouted to be heard over the roar of the engine, "Remember, Captain, you will not rise to the occasion; you will fall to the level of your training. Kenny, you had exceptional training! Go get those bastards!"

Kenny Junior got his P-40 Kittyhawk up into the sky. The American pilots, Welch and Taylor, also got their P-40s up and began shooting down any

Japanese Zero they could. Captain Kenny Schildmeyer fought bravely. Unfortunately, he was shooting down a Japanese bomber. Two A6M2s surprised him from above.

In the jungle east of Haleiwa, a group of small eyes watched through the jungle canopy as the first wave of Japanese planes retreated back to their carriers.

Pearl Harbor...

The carnage the second wave of zeros left behind was unbelievable. Pearl Harbor was ablaze. Thick smoke made it nearly impossible for the third Japanese wave of planes to see their targets, and it was called off. Not sending that wave would be the greatest Japanese regret.

Maili was doing her best to console Sommy as they viewed the damage from the upstairs balcony.

Sommy was still crying when she saw Savita on the grass. "No! No! No, Savita!"

Maili ran down to give aid to her loyal guard. His machine gun, still in hand, had spent all of its rounds. Savita had taken a round from friendly fire to the chest and died instantly.

The horrors of the day were just beginning.

Lizzy ran to Maili in hysterics, "Maili! Kenny's plane was shot down over the ocean!"

Maili's anger forced her to grit her teeth so tightly that she nearly chipped a tooth and said, "No, Lizzy! Did they see a parachute?"

Lizzy, "I don't know. Ryan is driving out there now to look for him and the kids."

"Can you come with me and Sommy to Pearl, and then we will head to Haleiwa?"

The three wahines got into the royal vehicle and sped to Pearl Harbor in search of Sommy's son, then to find the twins and the rest of the Schildmeyers.

The jungles east of Haleiwa...

Izzy looked around and said, "The skies have been clear for some time. I think if another wave was coming, it would have happened by now." He looked at Tatu and said, "Let's get the kids home."

Charlie asked, "Is Kenny ok?"

Emily responded, "I don't know, sweetheart. I am sure all the pilots will head home as soon as possible." The children and Izzy decided to attempt a car ride back to the palace.

After an anxious ride that approached the gates of Pearl Harbor, the US military blocked the road, saying, "I am sorry, sir, no one can pass."

Izzy got out of the car and said, "We have the princesses. They need to get back to the palace."

The MP said, "It just so happens the queen is right over there talking with the admiral."

Izzy and Tatu drove the vehicles to the edge of the water. Thick, black smoke still filled the air. Firemen were hosing down burning ships. The once-beautiful bay was filled with oil, dead bodies, and listed ships.

Bethany and Elizabeth got out first and rushed to Maili. Lizzy saw Charlie and Hannah and ran to embrace them. Emily had to yell over the commotion, "Mother, Kenny left us to fly his plane!"

Lizzy's eyes filled with tears. "He was shot down over the water. We don't know his status. Father has gone to find out."

Sommy hugged the girls and said, "I am so glad you are okay. I couldn't bear to lose another one today."

Bethany asked, "Why are you here?"

Sommy pointed to *Arizona*. She couldn't say it.

Bethany slowly fell to her knees. Oh my God, is that *Arizona*? Was Tutu on board?"

Sommy began to cry again as she shook her head.

Maili pulled Izzy and Tatu over to speak privately. Holding back her emotions, she said, "Savita was killed today as well. He was shot while defending the palace."

Izzy and Tatu looked at each other. Izzy placed his hand on Tatu's back as they rubbed their eyes. "Damn. Poor Savita. He's got a wife and kids."

Maili gathered everyone around and said, "Today has been the worst day of our lives. However, the Japanese may return. The admiral expects an invasion. We must do what we can to help. We are not soldiers, but we can help the nurses. We are going to the local hospital. I must warn you of what you are about to see. Burn victims. Young men with limbs shot off I need you stronger than you have ever been. The kingdom and these brave American sailors need us." They all shook their heads in agreement.

Niihau ...

Pilot Nishikaichi's Zero was running low on fuel. Izzy and Tatu's aim was better than he expected. He was instructed by his superiors, if the pilots had fuel or engine problems, to land their plane on Niihau, and a submarine would appear at night to pick him up.

Nishikaichi decided to land in a barren field. The natives had been warned that Japanese pilots might use their fields, so they had plowed them over to make a safe landing impossible.

A ranch hand saw the crash and came to the pilot's aid. Nishikaichi spoke a little English and, in his shock, allowed the ranch hand to take his pistol and paperwork.

Sommy's husband, Afa, had just landed on Niihau. Afa had been given permission to visit his cousin

Ben Kanahele and his wife Ella, as Niihau is a private island known as *the Forbidden Island*".

No one on Niihau had heard about the attack on Pearl Harbor yet and didn't fear the pilot. That night, the islanders decided to have a luau for their two new visitors.

Nishikaichi tricked the islanders, and in the middle of the night, after most people were intoxicated, he stole back his pistol along with a shotgun.

As the villagers awoke the next morning, a radio station alerted the villagers, and some escaped on a boat to Kauai to bring back the owner of the island, Mr. Robinson. Feeling he was going to be found by the Americans, Nishikaichi threatened the villagers. Ben had enough and ran at the pilot. Nishikaichi shot Ben three times, but he managed to knock Nishikaichi down. Afa kicked away his shotgun as Ella grabbed a boulder and smashed Nishikaichi in the head. Ben pulled out his knife and ended the fight permanently.

Chapter 35 - The War Effort

US Military Hospital, Pearl Harbor, December 8, 1941

Queen Maili and her twins, along with the Schildmeyers, had worked 20 straight hours. Soldiers, sailors, and civilians continued to be rolled into the hospital.

The rooms, the floors, and the waiting rooms were packed with bloody, broken, and burned humans. The royals had no nursing experience, but everyone could help clean and comfort the suffering. Bethany and Elizabeth were on gurney patrol. Men came in on the verge of death and were often later placed back on the gurney in body bags. The twins rolled them to the back of the hospital and tried their best to gently place them on the ground. They pushed the gurney back into the hospital or waited for an ambulance to do it all over again.

Head Nurse Nancee Mathor gathered the group together. "I can see through the window that the sun is coming up. You all need to go home and get plenty of sleep. We would love to have you back, Your Majesty, but only after some sleep and a good meal. It has slowed enough for now."

Maili, exhausted, agreed.

"If the Japanese do invade, we may have to do this all over again." Nancee noted.

The group of family and friends hugged and held each other as they left together. James gritted his teeth and said, "I hate the Japanese, Mother! I am going to enlist tomorrow! I will avenge Kenny and all these men who suffered today."

Lizzy put her arm around her only son and said, "I appreciate your passion, James, but you are our only son now. You can help the war effort and stay at home, don't you think?"

"We are at war, Mother. I am fighting for Kenny, for freedom, and for you, My Queen." James said it passionately and patriotically.

Lizzy said, "Bless you, James. I am too tired to think now. Perhaps we need to rest, eat, and then have this discussion tonight.

As they arrived at the palace, a telegram was waiting. Queen Maili opened it up.

Dear Queen Maili,

My condolences to you, Maili, and the Hawaiian people for all that you have gone through these past 24 hours. I want you to know that the United States declared war on Japan today. I commit to doing anything you need to help restore and rebuild Pearl Harbor. We are shipping medical supplies, food, and weapons to you and all of your islands immediately.

With your permission, the Navy will place Marines and anti-aircraft guns on every island. We will also increase naval support, which will include submarines. Please ensure that all of your chiefs will support our troops and inform all of your ship captains to fly their flags so they are not accidentally sunk.

I promise you, Your Majesty, we will avenge you.

Sincerely,

Franklin D. Roosevelt, President of the United States

Maili folded up the letter and placed it in her bloodstained pocket.

Maili encouraged everyone, "Let's drink some water, have a quick bite, and get some sleep. We all need and deserve it. I was so proud of all of you today. I would like to get back to the hospital by 6 PM to give the nurses some relief."

The families dragged themselves up the stairs and could barely make it to their rooms. Bethany tugged on Elizabeth's dress and said, "This is what the gods were trying to tell us."

"I was thinking the same thing. I wonder what dying on the beaches and in cities touched by the sun means, "Bethany asked.

Elizabeth teared up: "I don't know, but I have a feeling it's horrible."

Chapter 36 - The War Pendulum Swings

The Western Pacific, 1942

On April 18, 1942, on the deck of the USS Hornet, several B-25s were getting ready for takeoff on a secret mission. The war had just begun, but the Americans were desperate for a victory to rally support.

This mission was to take place a few hundred miles east of Tokyo. James Doolittle was about to change the course of the war. His 16 bombers left the aircraft carrier bound for an industrial area of Tokyo. The message: "We're coming!"

Japan had been invading Asian countries and Pacific islands for years. Today, war will come to the people of Japan. With no warning, multiple factories were destroyed, and over 50 people were killed and over 400 wounded. It would be just the beginning for the Japanese people.

Sommy interrupted the queen's conversation with Lizzy, saying, "Excuse me, My Queen, I have great news! Doolittle's raid was successful! Tokyo was bombed by 16 B'25s."

Maili hugged Lizzy and said, "Sommy, that is outstanding news. The Japanese woke up a sleeping giant and infuriated a motivated queen."

On June 4, the Japanese and American naval forces were searching for each other somewhere north of Hawaii. Queen Maili was observing a group of soldiers in the Communications Center. They looked Hawaiian, but she did not recognize them.

Ryan Schildmeyer had been working closely with Major Woodrow Defont and Captain Steve Bollard. "Your Majesty, there are some men I want you to meet." The Queen and Ryan approached Major Defont.

"Ryan, good to see you. We've had a tremendous breakthrough today."

"Woody, I'd like to introduce you to Queen Maili." Ryan made a hand gesture to approach.

Defont bowed and said, "Your Majesty, we have great news. Corporal Etsitty and Private Patrick Partz are working as one of our 'code talkers'.

Maili asked, "What's a code talker?"

"They all speak fluent Navajo. It is a remote Indian tribe in the American Southwest, and we are positive the Japanese will never break our codes.

We recently broke their code, so we finally know where they are."

Corporal Lightcloud Etsitty turned towards the queen, stood, and bowed, "Aloha, Your Majesty. We finally broke the Japanese code. Our plan now is to wait until their planes go into their carriers to refuel. That way, they won't have protection as we send in dive bombers and torpedo planes. We hope to sink them all. These are the carriers that launched the attack on Pearl."

"That makes me extremely happy." Relief and joy passed across Maili's face.

Captain Bollard spoke, "We know they want Midway. It has a great landing strip and oil containers. We are setting the trap to let them get close enough to strike with all the aircraft the United States could provide."

Just then, Communications Clerk Betty Shaffer delivered an important telegram.

Defont pumped his fist. "The plan worked. The Navajo Code Talkers provided the information the admirals needed from the USS Yorktown, the USS Enterprise, and the USS Hornet."

The pendulum of war had just swung back toward the Americans. Japan was forced to think of the war from a defensive position. All four Japanese carriers—the Akagi, Kaga, Soryu, and Hiry—were lost, including 300 aircraft and 2,500 men.

The Americans sadly lost one carrier, the USS Yorktown. The loss of 300 men and 145 planes was an extreme and costly sacrifice, but it was worth it. Maili had mixed emotions. Part of her was happy to get her revenge. Part of her was overwhelmed by sadness over the loss of lives and the impact on the families in America. And part of her thought of Hideki—where would he be if he were alive? Which side would he have chosen?

August 7, 1942, began the American strategy of "Island Hopping" at Guadalcanal. The plan was to remove the Japanese from the hundreds of islands they had taken over the last decade until American bombers could destroy all of Japan's manufacturing and limit their ability to produce weapons.

James Schildmeyer's battle experience was heroic but brief. After three days of fighting on the nearby island of Tulagi, James received shrapnel from a grenade that pierced his kneecap, preventing him from using his right leg effectively. James was awarded the Purple Heart by the US Military and sent back to Oahu. There, he served four years in the weapons department, serving Hawaii as a clerk. Bethany's foreshadowing came true, as thousands of American and Hawaiian boys lay dead on beaches all over the Pacific.

The island-hopping strategy cost thousands of young Americans' lives, but the end of the war could be seen. The Japanese were losing battle after battle.

Princess Bethany and Princess Elizabeth, along with their best friends Emily and Charlie, became candy stripers. They spent nearly every day treating wounded soldiers. As the war raged on, thousands of wounded streamed into Oahu. The girls did the work of angels: changing bandages, feeding men, changing bedpans, and entertaining the troops. Bethany felt that her dance lessons paid off as she performed for the troops on multiple occasions.

The four wahines became extremely popular with the American troops. Looking into Bethany's and Elizabeth's eyes became the highlight of most soldiers' days. The girls could not believe how young some of these boys were. Many were barely 18 years old.

On October 10, Maili received another telegram. This one was from England. Maili and the twins were conversing around the dinner table, finishing up dessert, when Sommy entered the room and handed her the telegram. Maili read to herself.

Queen Maili,

With the deepest regret, I need to inform you that Prince Austen was killed in a bombing raid in London. The Department of Defense wanted you to know that he died heroically. He ran out of the bomb shelter to assist a mother and her children, and they were trapped outside as the bombs fell.

My sincere condolences,

Your old friend,

Queen Elizabeth

Maili looked upward and quietly said, "Why, God? Why?" She dropped the telegram on the table and left to go to her room.

Bethany grabbed the telegram and read it: "Oh my God, Elizabeth, Father is dead!"

Chapter 37 - The Bloody War Ends in Europe

US Military Headquarters, Pearl Harbor, May 3, 1945

Queen Maili, Princess Bethany, Princess Elizabeth, Ryan Schildmeyer, and Walt Underson were summoned to US military headquarters. Rumors swirled about tremendous news.

Bethany asked, "What do you think this is about, Mother?"

Elizabeth interrupted, "I bet it's about Hitler! We've been in the media blackout for so long, I bet he surrendered."

Walt spoke up: "I bet you a coconut he did not surrender." Elizabeth shook his hand.

Maili looked at the girls and said, "Please get serious and pay attention," as she gave Walt a serious look.

Admiral Nimitz and General Short proudly marched in as the military personnel in the room stood at attention.

General Short looked at the Admiral for approval, and he began to speak: "Your Majesty, there is gratifying and devastating news. We apologize for the media blackout, but what we are about to say will change the outcome of the war." He looked at Admiral Nimitz again and said, "Your Majesty, President Roosevelt passed away a few days ago."

The group gasped and started to grumble.

Short continued, "Vice President Truman has been sworn in as our new president, and the government is running smoothly, as expected."

Maili inhaled deeply and said, "I am shocked to hear the news. I will be in contact with President Truman and Eleanor as soon as possible."

Admiral Nimitz cleared his throat and said, "I do have spectacular news, Your Majesty! Just last week, both Benito Mussolini and Adolf Hitler were killed!"

The room burst into applause. The crowd began hugging, laughing, and crying.

Nimitz continued, "Yes, we are all thrilled. Hitler committed suicide in his bunker with his wife Eva Braun before fellow Italians brutally murdered Mussolini.

Walt looked at Elizabeth and said, "You owe me a coconut."

Elizabeth asked, "Who would want to marry that madman?"

Maili asked, "What is to become of Germany and Italy?"

Short replied, "That is to be determined. The world will never quite be the same, and it appears Stalin is pushing his troops well into Europe. If he doesn't stop, we may have a new enemy."

Elizabeth raised her voice and asked, "What is the matter with these leaders? Isn't six years of war enough?"

Short shot back: "Dear Princess, we hope he only wants to ensure the Nazis are wiped out. The Russian people have suffered greatly. Like us, he wants revenge. Reports are coming in that the Soviet Army has already begun to escalate troops eastward to assist in the fight against Japan."

Walt was the political advisor for the queen and said profoundly, "Your Majesty, Italy has already begun to rebuild their new government, and I assume a post-Hitler Germany will do the same."

Queen Maili looked at Ryan and Walt and asked, "Does the Soviet expansion eastward mean the war in Asia is expanding?"

Walt raised his hand again and said, "This should expedite the war's ending, Your Majesty."

General Short pulled down a map of Eastern Asia and said, "We believe the Soviets will push the remaining Japanese troops out of Manchuria and Korea. This will occupy the fascist Japanese there while we prepare our invasion of Honshu, the main island of Japan."

Bethany gasped, "America is going to invade Japan? Won't that mean tens of thousands of deaths? My dream of men dying on the beach She said it in disbelief.

General Short used his pointer to direct the room's attention to Iwo Jima and Okinawa. "That has been happening for some time, Princess. We have already lost over 6,000 Marines on Iwo Jima. The losses after a month at Okinawa look to be extremely devastating on the US side. What is more disturbing is the change of tactics by the Japanese. First, they fought to the last man on Iwo Jima. Current Japanese death numbers are 18,000. On Okinawa, they have started using their planes as suicide bombers on our ships. They conscripted every healthy man because they believe Okinawa to be Japanese territory, and the death numbers are staggering on both sides."

Maili shook her head and said, "This is so tragic."

"We expect total losses on both sides to approach 200 to 300,000 by the end of the year!"

Bethany shouted, "Why doesn't the Emperor surrender? Doesn't he love his people?"

General Short consoled the princess, saying, "Hirohito has military advisors that are telling him he can still win this war. We hope to begin daily bombing raids on Japan once the Okinawa airstrip is under our control. Within a few weeks, their factories and refineries will be obliterated. However, we have intercepted transmissions going out to all Japanese citizens saying, "Be prepared to fight to the death for the emperor and Japan."

Elizabeth asked, "So they are going to have old men, women, and children fighting American troops?"

"It appears that way, Your Majesty!" Short replied.

Maili walked over to the map and stared. "We have bombers that can reach Japan and return to Okinawa."

General Short pointed out the window and said, "The first ones arrived yesterday. They are B-29s. They can fly higher than Japanese fighter planes or artillery can reach. So they don't even need machine guns for defense. We will be able to destroy all of their factories within weeks. We also have new incendiary bombs. These bombs have fuel that burns down buildings and creates 'firestorms'!"

Maili asked, "Firestorm?"

We first tried this in a German manufacturing city called Dresden in February. The flames from the bombs created such heat that they created storm-force winds. This condition fanned the flames to a point where they created their own storm, called a firestorm. The entire city burned down. Over 100,000 people died. We wanted to show Hitler that it was futile to resist. Hitler didn't relent. We hope Emperor Hirohito will."

Bethany looked at Elizabeth and said, "My dream! Cities on fire!"

Elizabeth said, "Oh my God!"

Maili continued to look at the map. "General, when will this nightmare end?"

"Our hope is for their surrender before the invasion. My best guess is this fall, Your Majesty."

Chapter 38 - The Sun Touched the Earth

The White House, Washington, D.C., July 17, 1945.

President Harry S. Truman was sitting in the Oval Office. An urgent telegram was delivered to his desk. President Truman opened it and read it to his wife.

Aloha, President Truman,

I apologize that we have never met. President Roosevelt and I had met on several occasions, and I send my condolences to you and the United States on his passing months ago.

After meeting with General Short and Admiral Nimitz, I implore you to end this war before the invasion of the Japanese island of Honshu takes place.

On behalf of all of the people of Hawaii, please exhaust every means of diplomacy. It pains me to think of so many civilians who will perish should an invasion occur.

May your God give you the wisdom to end this war immediately, and I am hopeful I can meet face-to-face with you and your lovely wife Bess in the upcoming days. Aloha.

Sincerely,

Queen Maili Grace Baitmen Kaanapali

"Bess, I need to confide in you something that is of the utmost importance. Queen Maili is right. We need to end the suffering immediately."

Bess touched his shoulder gently and asked, "What can I do for you, Mr. President?"

"I'm just plain ol' Harry, Bess. Yesterday, our scientists tested a bomb they called 'The Gadget'. It's a damn stupid name for something so horrific." Harry paused and stared at the portrait of George Washington. "Bess, it was an atomic bomb. It gets its power by splitting atoms, a power never known to man before."

"I'm not a scientist, Harry. What does that mean?"

"It is more powerful than anything ever created. Einstein and Oppenheimer created it. It gets as hot as the surface of the sun. One bomb can devastate an entire city, killing tens of thousands of people within seconds. This includes civilians." His voice trailed off: "Bess."

"How long have we had this bomb, Harry?"

"I learned about it a few days after Franklin passed away. The first successful test was yesterday in Alamogordo, New Mexico. I spoke with Mr. Oppenheimer myself. It worked better than expected."

Bess thought for a moment, "Are you going to use an atomic bomb on Tokyo?"

"No, Bess, a smaller city with military importance. We want the emperor to be around so the people of Japan will submit to our will through his commands. Plus, we are worried about Stalin. The Soviets will probably try to take Korea. This might persuade Stalin not to be aggressive after the war ends. I have to give the final approval for the military to drop it."

"Well, dear, I have two questions. Will it end the war, and will it save American lives?"

"I'd wager yes on both accounts," Harry answered his wife.

Bess looked into Harry's eyes and said, "I agree with Queen Maili too. End the war as soon as possible. They started it, and we will finish it!"

Two weeks later...

Even though Bethany was 25, she still had horrendous nightmares. Her visions continued to come true during World War II. Tonight would be the worst she'd ever had.

Bethany was flying again. She was so high that the air was freezing cold. She caught up to a metallic silver aircraft. She looked down and saw a large island below. It was much larger than Hawaii's Big Island. Bethany did not recognize the island. The plane had the name of a lady on the front: *Enola Gay*.

The princess could not shake the intense cold. The bomb bay doors opened, and a single bomb fell. The bomb was humongous. A small parachute opened and appeared to slow down the bomb. The *Enola Gay* dove and flew far away from Bethany.

Instantly, Bethany was on the ground on the outskirts of the city limits. The sign read *Hiroshima*. Birds by the thousands were flying away from the city. "How strange?" she thought. Bethany could see pamphlets on the ground that warned the people that a large bomb was about to be dropped. It was written in Japanese, but somehow Bethany could read it. Then the bomb ignited. It was silent. The flash was so intense that it appeared as if the sun had touched Hiroshima. Just like in her previous dream. Bethany was blinded, but in her mind's eye, she could see what had happened to the city.

People disintegrated instantly, leaving only their shadows on the sidewalks and buildings. An explosion of intense heat followed and swept quickly through the city. The intense heat melted people's skin, and their eyes exploded in their heads. Farther out from the hypocenter, 500 mph winds blew bricks, nails, cars, humans, and building debris into thousands of other people, killing them quickly.

As the smoke began to clear, Hiroshima was gone. 40,000 people, mostly civilians, died in seconds. They were the fortunate ones. Hundreds survived the initial blast, but they did not perish quickly. What was left of their melted skin gave them the appearance of eyeless zombies. In a state of shock, thousands attempted to stand, shuffle, or crawl in search of help.

Bethany awoke! She let out a blood-curdling scream. Maili and Elizabeth ran into her room, followed quickly by Sommy.

"Sweetheart, what is the matter?" Maili noticed Bethany's skin appeared red, as if she had suffered severe sunburn.

"Mother! Mother! I can't see! I can't see!"

Maili ran to her bedside and said, "Bethany, I am right here."

Bethany calmed herself: "Mother, in my dream, I saw a horrendous flash. I looked at it for just a second, and I became blind. My skin is burning, Mother!"

Maili looked at Sommy with dread and said, "Sommy, please get a doctor here immediately!"

Elizabeth sat by her sister and asked, "Elizabeth, what happened in your dream?"

"Elizabeth, I saw the sun touch a city. The city was called Hiroshima. Everyone died from just one bomb. They were burned and incinerated. It was just... horrible."

A few hours later...

A team of doctors and their private nurse, Dana, had rushed to give aid to Bethany. An ophthalmologist looked into Bethany's eyes as a dermatologist was treating her burns and said, "I have seen this before with children, but never with an adult. Princess, did you stare at the sun recently?"

"No doctor."

Maili told the doctor, "She was fine when she went to bed, Doctor Scott. This happened last night."

The doctor stated, "Staring at the sun usually causes this. The good news is that there appears to be no permanent damage. Her sight should return to normal in a few days."

The dermatologist, Dr. Alora Denay, agreed: "It appears that somehow the princess was exposed to intense sunlight. Did you lay out in the sun yesterday with your eyes open, by any chance?"

Elizabeth became aggravated: "Doctors! We were together all day yesterday. I'm fine. This happened in her dream!" Her dreams were a closely guarded secret. Nurse Dana confirmed Elizabeth's claim.

The doctors looked at each other with curiosity and said, "Princess, dreams don't burn you; heat does."

Maili calmed Elizabeth down: "I am sure you are correct, doctors. We will ensure the princess gets plenty of rest out of the sun until you say she can go outside again."

Dr. Garrett Scott said, "Let's keep her eyes covered for 48 hours. I will return then and do another exam. Dana, can you please ensure she keeps these on? Her eyes need rest, darkness, and time to heal. Dana nodded. The doctors left Bethany's room, not knowing what to think.

Maili sternly said to Elizabeth, "Let's try to keep Bethany's dreams to ourselves from now on."

"Yes, Your Majesty, my apologies," Elizabeth said.

Dana leaned into Bethany and said, "You will be just fine, My Princess, if you follow the doctor's orders."

The royal butler, Jordan, appeared with breakfast. "Where should I leave this, Your Majesty?"

"Oh, please leave it by the door, and we will get to it in a moment. Mahalo, Jordan."

Jordan bowed and said, "It is my pleasure, Your Highnesses. I'm praying for a speedy recovery, Princess Bethny," and he left the room.

General Short knocked on Bethany's door and marched in, saying, "Your Majesties, I have..." The general stopped in his tracks and said, "Oh my God, what happened to Princess Bethany?"

Maili responded, "The doctors are not sure. But the good news is they think her sight will return in a few days."

"She's... blind?"

Bethany responded, "It's temporary, according to the eye doctor."

"Oh my. I am so sorry, Princess. Well, maybe this will help brighten your spirits. The war is closer than ever to being over, Your Majesties. We used a new weapon on"

Bethany interrupted the general, saying, "You dropped a sun bomb on Hiroshima, didn't you?" Maili looked at her, clearly irritated.

The general was flabbergasted. "How did you know that, Princess? That was our military's most guarded secret."

"Can I tell him, Mother?" Bethany asked.

"Well, General, you'd better sit down. Sommy, grab him a chair, please."

Bethany sat up and winced from the pain of her burns. "General, in my dream last night, I saw the sun drop on Hiroshima. It was more horrific than I can say. The plane was called the *Enola Gay*. It was one of those B-29s."

General Short was in shock. "How could you have possibly known that? I didn't even know until an hour ago. It's not a sun bomb; it is an atomic bomb, but similar in outcome."

"I have very real and strange dreams. This one was the strangest and most real. I was there, General. I saw the atomic bomb detonate. I looked at it, and now I can't see. The entire town was destroyed. Thousands of people are now dead. Killed by one bomb."

"You are correct, Princess Bethany." General Short stared at the queen with suspicion.

"You do not believe my daughter, General? Bethany does not lie!"

"I don't know what I believe, Your Majesty. However, we are all hopeful that this will pressure the emperor to surrender soon."

Maili sighed. "Let's all pray that he does."

Chapter 39 - Japan Surrenders

The Deck of the USS Missouri, September 2, 1945

Emperor Hirohito, along with his people, had suffered enough. Nearly three million Japanese had died or been casualties of the worst war in the history of the planet.

Even after the devastation of Hiroshima, Japan did not capitulate. Kokura was the next target city; however, cloud cover prevented the bombing of that city. *The B-29 Box Car* went to its second target.

Unfortunately, President Truman felt that this forced him to drop another atomic bomb on the city of Nagasaki. This bomb was called *Fat Man.* The sun would touch another city, resulting in the deaths of well over 60,000 people.

On September 2, 1945, World War II would officially end. Hundreds of diplomats from around the Pacific gathered on the deck of the great battleship *USS Missouri.* Even Ryan Schildmeyer was present, representing Hawaii.

Ryan leaned over to General Short and said, "This is amazing! The world's leaders are getting together to promote peace."

"Indeed, Ryan."

Hundreds of US bombers flew over Tokyo with their bomb bay doors open as a sign they would not drop any more bombs, but their sheer numbers clearly stated they could.

Unbeknownst to the diplomats at the ceremony, three radical Japanese pilots were attempting to take off from a local airstrip. Their goal was a kamikaze attack on the deck of the *USS Missouri* to kill as many military leaders and politicians as possible. Doing so would have brought untold wrath upon the Japanese survivors. Luckily for the world, Emperor Hirohito got word and drove quickly to the airport. He begged the pilots not to go, and they complied.

Several weeks later...

Bethany, who was fully recovered, Elizabeth, and Maili were on the patio enjoying breakfast. "Mother," Princess Bethany asked, "what happens now to Japan and its people?"

Maili folded her newspaper and said, "They rebuild. Like we did after Pearl Harbor. They will slowly rebuild their cities. Their government will also start from scratch under the guidance of the United States as a democracy."

Elizabeth placed her fork down as she finished her pineapples and guavas and said, "My Queen, I do not trust Stalin and the Soviet Russians. They seem to be obtaining land at alarming rates. First Eastern Europe, and now Korea I also overheard some generals talking about how the Soviets were helping Mao Zedong in China. Wasn't he the communist who turned your friend Po into a madman?"

Maili took a deep breath and looked off into the distance. "Yes, Dear Princess, he was brainwashed. Poor Po."

"You never talk about Po or Hideki." Elizabeth inquired.

Lizzy interjected, "We were all great childhood friends, but they were casualties of their times. Politicians impact individuals, not just groups. Hideki was influenced by the fascists of Japan, and Po was influenced by the communists of China."

Maili looked at Lizzy with sadness and said, "Your aunt Lizzy and I had amazing childhoods. I feel so horrible about what the war did to so many children around the world. So, that leads me to our next discussion. I received two important letters recently."

"Who from, Mother?"

"Funny, you should ask Bethany. The first one was from a new international political body called the United Nations. It will open in New York. I have chosen you to speak on behalf of Hawaii, Princess."

"How exciting! Why me, Mother?" Bethany said it brightly.

"The speakers will be survivors of the Holocaust and nuclear blasts."

"But Mother, I wasn't there."

"Well, the cat is apparently out of the bag, because my other letter is from a survivor from Hiroshima and Nagasaki. His name is Tsutomi Yamaguchi. He heard your story and wants to meet you in New York at the United Nations. He too will be a speaker."

Bethany was astonished: "An actual survivor heard about my dream?"

"Apparently. He said your story was exactly what he experienced with partial blindness and severe sunburn."

Elizabeth said, "Wow, Bethany. You are going to be famous."

"Shoot, sister, I am already famous. My hula is known from here to Timbuktu." Bethany said it with a smile.

Lizzy asked, "My Queen, what can you tell us about this 'Holocaust' in Europe?"

"Oh, Lizzy, it is unbelievably sad. Hitler and the Nazis had been placing Jewish people and others they deemed inferior into concentration camps. The Nazis used them as slaves until the *Final Solution* occurred. Millions of people were murdered in those camps during the last months of the war, and their bodies were sent to crematoriums."

Bethany asked, "Didn't the Americans force the Japanese into camps in California?"

"Princess, I cannot justify what the Americans did, but the Japanese Americans were not slaves or murdered, thank God. Sadly, I had to send some

Japanese-Hawaiians there too. I am ashamed, but in war, leaders have to make horrible choices."

"I will certainly be willing to speak on behalf of peace and the horrors of nuclear bombs." Bethany said.

Chapter 40 - From a Hot War to the Cold War, with the Hopes of No War

Pearl Harbor, Oahu, Hawaii, May 3, 1946

Queen Maili, along with her entourage and several high-ranking military leaders of the United States, were touring the improved technologies of radar, sonar, and newer, more sophisticated weapons in and around Pearl Harbor.

"General, I have a better sense of safety knowing about the advanced weaponry, but I am puzzled about *Arizona.*" Maili's statement appeared melancholy.

"The American military would ask two favors of Your Majesty. We would like to make *the USS Arizona* the resting place for the 1,100 Americans entombed. We want to make it a cemetery for those men, and we would like to bury the thousands of men who gave their lives in the Pacific in an international cemetery in the Punchbowl. Would Her Majesty agree to that?"

"Oh, General and Admiral, of course. It would be our honor!"

When the war ended, thousands of World War II veterans had departed Hawaii for the last time as G.I.s, but they would often return as veterans with their new families to pay respects to those unfortunates who could not return. Hawaii, specifically Waikiki Beach in Honolulu city limits, brought millions of vacationers to Oahu. Princess Likelike's dreams had come to fruition.

The Generals did have concerns about Hawaii's future: "Queen Maili, we believe that the Soviet threat is growing daily. We believe Hawaii will always continue to provide a strong military component to the Pacific. President Truman and Congress have fully committed to providing defense for you, should you continue to have us here. Admiral Nimitz and General MacArthur are working to make Guam the 49th state."

"That is wonderful for the people of Guam." Maili said it happily.

"Has the queen ever contemplated Hawaii becoming the 49th or 50th state of the United States?" The general inquired.

"I have always loved and respected the relationship the United States and my kingdom have had, but my days of ruling are coming to an end. That would be something the princesses would be better at deciding than I would."

The general looked at the two beautiful twins and raised his eyebrows. "What do you think, princesses?"

Elizabeth turned to Bethany and said, "Perhaps we should discuss this in private counsel and get back to you, General."

"No rush, princesses. Just know I will always be at your service and more than willing to discuss such matters."

Ryan Schildmeyer asked the General, "What do you foresee happening to Europe, General?"

"My understanding is that the United States is going to pay for the reconstruction of Europe. There is a long road ahead for the West. The East appears to be under the 'care' of the Soviet Union. I dread to think about how those people will continue to suffer. I think Churchill put it best in his 'Iron Curtain' speech.

Sommy was trailing behind and asked, "Admiral, may I take a boat over to *Arizona to* pay respects to my son, Tutu?"

"Oh, goodness me, of course." He yelled for some seamen to assist Sommy.

Maili asked, "May I come too, Sommy?"

Sommy bowed, walked towards Maili, and whispered, "I love you, My Queen. Please come with me."

The two important passengers were shuttled out into the deeper water as their boat reached the rusting portions of metal; they were floating directly on top of the ship.

Tiny drops of oil wiggled their way up to the surface. The drops appeared to swim upward like tiny tadpoles made from oil. They stopped on the surface for a moment. Then, the droplets opened up like a blossom into a circular rainbow of colors as they bounced on top of the waves.

Sommy wept.

Maili asked the sailors, "How long will the oil continue to leak?"

One sailor said, "I heard *Arizona* has over one million gallons of fuel and oil, Your Majesty. I would project for decades."

"Sommy?" Maili asked with grief.

She regained her composure and said, "Yes, My Queen."

"I want you to know your son, and the other 1,000 men will not be forgotten. We will memorialize their sacrifice with a monument. I will ask Admiral Nimitz to help us begin the erecting of a memorial appropriate for what they sacrificed here."

Sommy leaned on the queen as she used her handkerchief to wipe away her tears. "Your Majesty, he was just a boy. Mommas should not have to bury their babies."

Maili wrapped her arm around Sommy's broad shoulders.

Back on the shore, a soldier caught Bethany's eye. Bethany asked Izzy to escort her to the line of soldiers on parade. The soldier saluted her, then stood at ease.

Elizabeth asked the Admiral, "How would we make Honolulu the port of call for your entire Pacific Fleet? I want to continue my Auntie Likelike's tradition of making Hawaii a tourist destination for the world."

"It would be an honor for me to ensure that the aloha spirit may kiss all American sailors." The admiral smiled—a rare event.

As Sommy paced along the shore, Elizabeth could see that she was distraught. Elizabeth ran to her second mother and said, "Oh, Sommy Honey, I know it is still so difficult."

"Princess, it's been more than four years, and it hurts like it was yesterday."

Maili asked the Admiral, "I want to assist in the building of a memorial appropriate for the sacrifices those men made here. What can Hawaii do?"

"Your Majesty, that is such an outstanding idea. I think we should visit Congress together and approach the Department of Defense with your idea." Maili smiled between her tears.

Bethany tapped her mother on the shoulder and said, "Mother, there is someone I think you should see."

"Oh, Princess, I am a mess right now." Bethany tugged at the queen's elbow until she reluctantly made her way over to a group of soldiers lined shoulder to shoulder. The man's face became recognizable. Maili quickened her pace.

"MAKA!"

Made in the USA
Monee, IL
02 November 2023

45610824R00174